more than saying
I LOVE YOU

ALSO BY ANDREA GOODMAN WEINER

The Best Investment: Unlocking the Secrets of Social Success for Your Child

more than saying
I LOVE YOU

Four Powerful Steps That Help
Children Love Themselves

Andrea Goodman Weiner, Ed.D.

FRANKLIN GREEN
PUBLISHING

Brentwood, Tennessee

MORE THAN SAYING I LOVE YOU
FRANKLIN GREEN PUBLISHING
P.O. Box 2828
Brentwood, Tennessee 37024
www.franklingreenpublishing.com

Cover design and illustrations by Olga Lopata

Library of Congress Cataloging-in-Publication Data
Weiner, Andrea Goodman, 1953-
  More than saying I love you : four powerful steps that help children love themselves / Andrea Goodman Weiner.
    p. cm.
  ISBN 978-0-9826387-8-1 (pbk. : alk. paper)
  1. Self-esteem in children. 2. Child rearing. I. Title.
  BF723.S3W446 2010
  649'.7—dc22
                                                        2010046440

Printed in the United States of America
1 2 3 4 5 6 7 8 9 10—15 14 13 12 11 10

This book is dedicated
in memory of
Chris Goodrich

A true Renaissance man

I love me. Who do you love?

Mary Midiri [1908–1990]

Born in Catania, Italy, Mary Midiri, the only daughter of Antonio and Vicenza Bertino, moved to South Philadelphia by way of Ellis Island when she was four years old. A hard worker with confidence to spare, Mary Midiri eloped to marry the man she loved, ran a corner candy store for more than forty years, raised four children, and spoiled her fourteen grandchildren. If you told Mary that her meatballs were to die for or that the stitches on the blanket she just crocheted were amazingly even, she would say, with a twinkle in her eye, "I love me. Who do you love?" Mary used that phrase without a lick of deceit whenever she was praised, which was often.

Contents

Acknowledgments

Writing a book is like giving birth. From the first spark of an idea, a book grows and develops in the author's mind. Then it progresses through the labor of writing, editing, and proofing to finally emerge as a complete work of love. There were many people whose efforts helped bring this book to fruition. I would like to thank Lee Gessner, my publisher, who believed that the message of the book was important enough to share with parents and caregivers. To my editor and project coordinator, Mary Sanford, whose critical eye for detail and common sense ideas added to the book and were much appreciated. Olga Lopata, my illustrator and cover designer, who took on this project with so much enthusiasm that she even sent me an "I Love Me" coffee cup. Thank you, Olga! Last but not least, Katherine Sansone, my publicist, whose organizational ability, candidness, integrity, and strong work ethic are just some of things I admire about her. She believed in this book from the very beginning, and I am indebted to her for her friendship, encouragement, great ideas, and art direction throughout this entire book-writing process.

I am deeply grateful for the many mentors of love—my "blue chips"—who have made invaluable contributions in my life. To Jeffery, my husband, for his unwavering support and love. His daily courage dealing with life challenges inspires me every day. For Aly, who has been my inspiration for the book and the joy in my life.

Watching her grow into an outstanding, loving young woman has been one of the best things any mother could experience. My brother Gary Goodman and his wife Kathy, who "always have my back" and who are always there for me. To my loving sister, Jane Preiser, who is steadfast in her support and makes me blush when she tells all of her friends how proud she is of her older sister. For my two brothers-in-law named David, I thank both of you for your support. To my two wonderful nieces, Jessica and Lexi, and my terrific nephew, Gregory, you make me feel like I'm the "coolest" aunt! Len and Madlyn Abramson, who are more than just family; you have been both important mentors and friends in my life. Laurie and David Yarock, my "newfound family," I'm so grateful for you both being in my life. Jean Weiner, the "youngest" acting matriarch of the family—your zest for life is an inspiration. My wonderful stepchildren: Doug and Rei Weiner, Hope and Gary Colen, Stacey and Quinn O'Brien—I love you all. And to the next generation, the grandchildren: Ben, Nate, Julia, Hannah, Ava, and Sydney, may you always have love and laughter in your lives.

Huge love and thanks to my "family" of friends: Michael Richardson, for your humor that keeps me laughing, your kindness, and your care for my family. I am so grateful for all of your help in so many ways. Lawrence Booth, I love your oversized Texan heart, which always reminds me of the goodness in people. Thank you for your generosity of spirit and for filling in the gaps in my life. Margaret Bledsoe, for all your help in keeping my life sane and on course, for your many words of encouragement, and for being a big part of Aly's life. You have my vote for when you become "Queen." Shelia Hedean, for your indomitable spirit, your love, and being a special guide in my life. You are truly a mentor of love! Judy Jacobson, my "soul sister," whose daily phone calls are my lifeline and who is one of the most fiercely loyal, honest, and fun friends I've been lucky enough to find in my life. Chandra Alexander, cousin and dear friend, our twenty-five years of friendship withstands the test of time. Thank you for keeping me "real." Jill Savin, an incredible example of what a good friend is; I am indebted to your support and optimistic attitude. Wendy Meagher, my "adopted" sister, who is always on the same wavelength as me. I am thankful for your influence in Aly's life and in mine as well. Mette Phillips, my dear friend whose daughter grew up with mine, your friendship and role of best cheerleader is so appreciated. Susan Eichert, my Pilates and golf buddy, I value our friendship and enjoy being in the same "club" as you, being moms to only daughters. Trish Baily, my island co-hort, who recognizes what I need and gives me the space to do it. Thank you for introducing Aly to the beauty of the sea and the need to keep it ecologically safe and pristine.

Prologue

College Application Question:

What was the best piece of advice you ever received? (500 words)

Answer:

The best piece of advice that I have ever been given is that if I love myself, I, in turn, can love others. This advice was given to me by my mother, who believes that loving yourself is the basis for developing good relationships throughout life. She would always tell me that even if she made a lot of mistakes as a parent, the "one gift" that she would have given me would be the ability to love myself, and thus, love others. As I approach my 18th birthday, I can now look back and know that this advice has helped me become more confident in myself, whether in an academic setting or in a social setting. I have been through many experiences in my life, and throughout the hardest times, this advice has helped me persevere.

When I love myself, it is a feeling that radiates and originates from my core and the deepest part of my being. It is learning how to express my uniqueness and appreciating whom I am from within. Loving myself is a journey that I now realize is something I will have to always nurture. Although my mother's lessons taught me how to love myself, I also saw the benefits through different milestones during my childhood and my adolescence. It helped me deal with unkind comments that mocked my appearance, my personality, and my family. I remember when I was six years old, a girl with dark hair in my class said, "Ew, you have yellow hair!" I then looked at her, and said, "I love my yellow hair, why wouldn't I?" Her reaction to my comment about my blonde hair was speechlessness, as I smiled at her, knowing that my hair was a part of me, and I loved every part of myself.

Another aspect of self-love is making wise and loving choices for yourself. This is something that I have especially learned during my adolescent years. As I watched my friends drink, do drugs, and party heavily, I chose not to partake in these activities because they would be hurtful and not loving to myself. I do not label these activities as universally "right" or "wrong," however, these choices were not for me. When you love yourself, you are able to stand in your truth, and by doing so, you can withstand peer pressure and negative comments.

The byproduct of loving myself is the confidence to take risks in doing beneficial things that I have never done before. The advice of loving myself will help me take the big leap into the next phase of my life, which is going to college. This relationship with myself will never cease, and as I mature throughout my life, this advice that I have used will only deepen and grow.

—Aly Weiner, December 2009

♡   ♡   ♡

As I read my daughter's essay, a feeling came over me. It was a feeling that occurs as a parent or even one who works closely with children when you realize that something you have been teaching them actually made an impact. It felt like a huge sigh of relief, but more than that, it was a sense of completion, and I admit I shed a few tears. As her words blurred in front of my eyes, I saw a flood of images of her, from the adorable infant she was—seemingly moments ago—to the beautiful young woman standing in front of me, watching as I read her answer.

"Mom, it really was the best advice I ever got," Aly said, as she noticed that my eyes were still glued to the paper. "I feel like it was so much a part of me that I'm not even sure how I learned it. How did you teach me how to love myself?"

"Aly," I said as I smiled and looked up at her, "it was a combination of many things that began even before you were born. It first started with a commitment. . . ."

more than saying
I LOVE YOU

Introduction

As a speaker and writer on the topic of the social and emotional well-being of children, I am often asked if an antidote exists for the widespread problem of bullying. Of course, this is a very complex as well as heart-wrenching issue, and the solution to it will take time and commitment on many different levels. But what is the root cause of bullying? Is it the higher rate of divorce? Is it because more parents are working, leaving them less able to supervise—or even spend time with—their children? Or what about technology? The widespread use of computers and cell phones seems to allow kids to disconnect from society. Does this disconnection encourage cyberbullying because kids think they "can't get caught" or that no one sees them being cruel? Have television and the movies gone too far with their portrayal of violence and sex, implying that it is "the norm"? Regardless of the answers to these questions, there is one truth that we can all agree on. Children are now living in a very complex world and are bombarded with external forces that generations before them did not have to contend with.

In addition to bullying, children today have to deal with any number of equally challenging issues such as teen pregnancy, depression, and alcohol and drug use. I believe that an antidote exists for all of these problems and more, and I also believe children are born with it.

Children are certainly not born with a pre-disposition to "be bad" or do hurtful things to others. Children are born loving. They do not know any different. They love themselves. They love everything, and they love unconditionally. They know nothing but love. Yet even though this inherent loving "spark" is within every individual, behaviors eventually appear that demonstrate a decided lack of love . . . toward oneself, which sometimes develops into not being loving toward others.

How did self-love become so elusive? What happens to that joyous bundle that starts out as nothing but love? These are questions that I have struggled with—especially when finding an answer became crucial for me when it came time for me to become a parent.

I was one of those women who put career first before starting a family. Before I gave birth to our daughter, Aly, I had already been through four successful careers: child and family therapist, business executive in the health care industry, junior interior decorator in New York City, and founder of a health care consultancy business. Yet, even with all of my life and business experience, I found myself panicking a month before I was to give birth to Aly. The idea that I was going to be completely responsible for another human being simply scared the living daylights out of me. With my background as a therapist, I was aware of all the technical and clinical aspects of parenting—what to do, what not to do. But knowing a lot about child development didn't mean I would never make mistakes. If anything, I might have known "too much," in terms of all that can go wrong! The bottom line was that I was afraid I would mess up being a parent to this innocent child who was due to be born in less than four weeks!

What eventually stopped my "panic attack" was a question I finally asked myself: "No matter how many mistakes you make as a parent, what would be the one 'gift,' or practical advice you could give her that she would be able to draw on for the rest of her life?" My answer was that if I could help her maintain that love for herself that she was born with, she could then develop the ability to love others. Although it sounded simple, I knew that this was the one "gift" I would commit to no matter what. Don't get me wrong: I wasn't sure how I was going to go about teaching her this. But the commitment I made that day allowed me to stop worrying (for the most part) and begin to enjoy the new adventure of parenthood.

We tell our children that we love them, and most of us believe that speaking those words will sustain self-love in our children or automatically create children who love themselves. We believe that if something is said over and over again it will gain validity and that our children will then internalize the daily "I love yous" and from that create self-love. It makes sense, but I know that it did not happen for me and for many other people that I know. Yet I grew up in a loving family. My family was kind and caring. My parents told me that they loved me. Still, even though I was secure in their love for me, I could not say that I loved myself. Growing up, I had friends, I did well academically in school, I was reasonably attractive, and I got along fairly well with my parents and siblings. I believe that I *liked* myself and thought I was "okay," but truly loving myself was not even an option. I thought that to be loved—even by myself— was not my inherent birthright; I had to *earn* it. I was so busy trying to earn other people's love that I never had time to simply appreciate me and love me for myself. This was something that I finally learned as an adult and even continued to learn as I taught my own child.

Does that mean that we have to wait until we grow up before we learn to love ourselves? I say no. It is my hope, and the premise of this book, that parents and other caregivers can learn to build a foundation for developing self-love, a love that will grow as our children mature into young adults.

Now, let's pause for a minute to clarify a very important point: loving oneself is not the same thing as being self-centered or egotistical. This is *not* a book about turning children into a generation of narcissists or demanding, selfish children. Narcissism is a personality disorder whose symptoms include believing you are better than others, exaggerating your own achievements or talents, failing to recognize other people's emotions or feelings, having trouble sustaining healthy relationships, and demanding special treatment to which you feel entitled. While it may seem that people who exhibit narcissistic traits have confidence or strong self-esteem, the reality is quite the opposite. Narcissists demand to have the best of everything—the best house, the best car, the best job. However, underneath these shallow shows of grandiosity is a very fragile self-esteem that comes from a place of fear, shame, and humiliation. Narcissists must react with rage or belittle others in order to feel like they look better.

So what would it look like to have a whole generation of children that successfully practiced loving themselves? They would be caring and loving toward others as well as themselves. Indeed, being able to love others as we love ourselves—or, as the Bible says, "love your neighbor as yourself"—comes from practicing self-love. They would appreciate their own talents and be accepting of who they are. By being accepting and compassionate toward themselves, they would in turn be the same way toward their friends, classmates, siblings, and parents. Their self-worth or high self-esteem would be a by-product of their self-love and would help build confidence and the courage to try and experience new things in life. Most importantly, when you can love yourself, you can make loving decisions for yourself and take prudent actions. This means questioning and refraining from overindulging in drugs and alcohol, sex before you are mature enough to handle it, unhealthy relationships that cause pain and hurt, and hurtful behaviors like bullying and humiliating others.

The book is divided into four steps to teaching self-love, each of which is keyed to a particular age group: Creating Internal Appreciation (birth to 5 years), Instilling Empathetic Acceptance (5 to 11 years old), Embracing Truth or Consequences (11 to 17 years old), and Living Loving Kindness (18 and older). I divided these steps into age categories because in my experience, most parents can relate easily to age groupings. However, this is by no means a rigid guideline. Parents of teenagers can certainly take some of the strategies discussed in steps one and two, which are designated for younger children, and adapt them to fit their needs. As children grow, their developmental needs change, and so do the different strategies used to reinforce self-love. The steps in this book build upon one another, and the approaches suggested can be continually reinforced.

This book is the culmination of my eighteen-year journey through the trials and tribulations of being a parent and also creating the most advantageous approaches to promote this important notion of children learning to love themselves. In learning how to promote self-love in my daughter, I learned and discovered the powerful lessons of loving *myself* along the way. Truly feeling self-love is the greatest accomplishment I could hope to achieve, and it is something that I know will keep expanding, fulfilling, and nourishing me for the rest of my life.

From my early commitment to teach this concept to my daughter, I have taken what I have learned and have shared many of the simple but powerful strategies that are discussed within each chapter with thousands of parents around the country. My motivation to finally write this book was ignited by a conversation I had with my daughter after I read an essay she wrote for one of her college applications. Aly's essay discussed what it meant to love oneself and how self-love helped her in her life. Having been raised with many of the strategies that are discussed in this book, she has never questioned the value of self-love—it's as natural as breathing to her. After I read her essay, she said to me, "Mom, I know I love myself, but how did *you* teach me this?" I felt that this was the opportunity to share with her not only my journey as a parent but also the steps I took to remind her of her birthright of love. To answer Aly's question, each chapter opens up with a "love letter" from me to my daughter that illustrates to her the different aspects of learning self-love. Within each chapter, there are additional exercises that will help parents and caregivers understand this concept even further, along with practical applications that you can use on a regular basis.

As Aly gets ready to celebrate her eighteenth birthday as a young adult and make the transition to college, I can happily feel that I have kept my commitment to her. I hope that this "gift" that I committed to giving my daughter almost eighteen years ago will be with her for the rest of her life. And with you, too, as you teach your children the joys of loving themselves.

Creating Internal Appreciation

Great Expectations

The moment a child is born, the mother is also born. She never existed before. The woman existed, but the mother, never. A mother is something absolutely new.

~RAJNEESH

Dear Aly,

Before you were born, I was already thinking about how I could give you the best life ever! One filled with many, many smiles, much laughter and happiness and as few tears, disappointments, and sadness as possible. Quite an undertaking for someone who only knew about children through babysitting (years ago), what I had observed from other parents, and of course, from working with families as a psychotherapist. All of these experiences were completely different from parenting my own child—trust me on that account! I would gaze at images of you from the ultrasounds, and I almost thought I could sense who you might be by feeling your movements inside my body. I read pregnancy books and magazines and learned about things I could do to encourage communication between us, such as having you listen to soothing music like Mozart or Vivaldi, and reading and talking to you daily. I even had your father "talk" to you so you would know his voice when you were born. He usually read to you from the sports page. (Our home baseball team wasn't doing well that year, so he had a lot to say!)

During my pregnancy, I found that it was calming for me to recite my wishes for you, so every day I would repeat, "Aly, listen very carefully . . ."

I want you to have a life filled with beauty, goodness, and truth in your life. I want you to be beautiful physically, emotionally, and spiritually.

No matter what happens in your life, you will never abandon your joy; remember to always be joyful and always spread joy.

You are going to be a really healthy baby, and you will stay healthy. You will accept no sickness and never be affected by disease.

You will by all means be truthful to your conscience, to the power of God within, and to the highest good and welfare to humanity.

You will be courageous and fearless and always stand in your truth. You will use your given talents to create your mission and purpose in life for the highest good for all.

You will be creative and bring with you inspiration from the higher realms. Your combined intellect and emotional well-being will always be in perfect balance.

Somehow I believed that if all of these wishes came true, your life would take a positive path with few regrets and only anticipation for more to come. Looking back over your life, I am thrilled to see that most of my wishes have come true, with the remaining ones yet to be part of your destiny.

I have to admit that about a month before you were born, I started to panic. The reality hit me that in just one month's time, I was going to be a full-fledged parent. Even with, or maybe even because of, all of my education and knowledge about child development, I knew full well what could go "wrong" with children because of parental issues and mistakes. As you are well aware, I am a bit of a perfectionist; it won't surprise you to learn that I didn't want to make any mistakes! Over time, I have learned that making mistakes as a parent goes with the

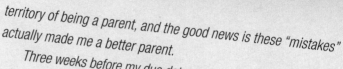

territory of being a parent, and the good news is these "mistakes" actually made me a better parent.

Three weeks before my due date, with all of these thoughts going through my head, a question came to me: What would be the one thing, the one gift, that as your mom I could give you that you would have for the rest of your life? The answer came to me in a rush, as if someone was whispering in my ear. My gift would be to teach you how to love yourself. I wanted you to learn self-love at an early age, allowing it to be a foundation for everything else in your life. I felt that if you could love yourself, you would love others in turn. Then I realized something: Here I was, at that time almost thirty-nine years old, and I wasn't even sure I could claim that for myself. Sure, I liked myself well enough, but did I really, truly love myself? I wasn't exactly sure how I was going to teach you self-love, but I sensed that this journey was going to be as important for me as it was for you. I believed that the "how to" aspect would present itself to me as long as I was committed to you learning this.

Now that I had made this commitment and had a goal and some direction as a parent, my anxiety and fears lessened and I felt a bit more ready for your arrival. I was now ready to be a mother (as ready as anyone thinks they can be!) and take on the full responsibilities of being a parent. You must have sensed this, since you decided to come two weeks earlier than expected! And when I gave birth to you and held all six and a half pounds of you in my arms, I felt a type of love that I had never expected or experienced before. Holding you in my arms, with your father next to me looking at you, we whispered softly to you the words, "Welcome, little one." Your reaction surprised us: you opened your blue eyes and smiled up at us as if you were welcoming us! I took your newborn grin as a sign that we were all going to be fine and that the journey ahead of us was definitely going to be a wonderful adventure!

Love,
Mommy

*M*uch research has been conducted on the factors that influence a baby in utero. From a physical perspective, proper nutrition, rest, and exercise can provide the essential conditions necessary for a healthy pregnancy. But mothers-to-be should also concentrate on bonding with their baby in utero in order to significantly improve the maternal/fetal connection while pregnant. Just like doing all the physical things to create a healthy infant, communicating with the baby during pregnancy helps build the foundation for a strong parent/child connection. The first step is talking to your baby as much as possible. Sometimes it helps if you use a nickname for the baby, or if you know the gender of the baby, as we did, you may have already settled on a name beforehand. Regardless of whether you know the gender or have a name picked out for the baby, research has shown that babies are comforted by the sound of their mother's voice. It is also a great idea to establish a bond with the child's father by having him talk to the baby in utero as well. Simply reading out loud from a newspaper, magazine, or book allows the connection to be made. Once born, infants tend to recognize their parents' voices right away and prefer their voices over strangers'.

One thing both parents can talk about is wishes for their unborn child. By reciting a list of wishes, parents can communicate to their baby words that are meaningful to them through visualizing positive outcomes for their child. By writing down your wishes for your child, you begin to define a "plan of action" that you wish to achieve for your soon-to-be-newborn. Whether or not these outcomes eventually come true is not as important as firming up your beliefs and aspirations—as a couple—for your child. By communicating these intentions, you can feel more connected to your unborn child and reinforce a loving bond with him or her.

Playing and listening to calming music is another approach to strengthen the parent/fetal bond. In fact, from at least the twenty-third week of pregnancy, a baby's hearing is developed enough to respond to outside noise. Take time each day to listen to your favorite music, whether it be classical or jazz. Some research suggests that soft music, such as classical or nature sounds, has a calming effect, while louder music may startle the baby. During my pregnancy, I played different kinds of classical music, such as Vivaldi and Mozart, as well as other kinds of music that I found soothing. After my daughter was born, she responded to the same music. Taking time out to enjoy the music creates a harmonious environment that also benefits the mother. The calmness that comes from enjoying the music ends up benefiting the baby as well. Studies have shown that the baby is affected by the mother's emotions via the hormones associated with them. The more relaxed and happy the mother feels, the happier the baby.

One of the things I did during my pregnancy was to be cognizant of the effects emotions or stress-producing events could have on my unborn daughter. Although my emotions could not cross the placenta, I knew that hormones could. When a mother becomes overly stressed, hormones called catecholamines are released, which have been to shown to affect emotions, especially fear and anger. These hormones could cross over into the placenta and disturb the developing fetal nervous system. Although short-term emotional upsets in pregnancies do not harm the baby emotionally, studies have shown that extreme emotional distress in mothers can produce anxious babies. Emotions, positive or negative, are more intense during pregnancy. When you realize that your own emotional health is connected to your baby's, you are more motivated to try and resolve those stresses in your life in a positive fashion so you can be sure your baby has the best emotional start.

Creating a strong bond with your baby before it is born is the first step in laying the foundation for developing a positive relationship with your child. Through communicating with your baby in utero—from singing, talking, creating positive intentions, listening to soothing music, and dealing effectively with emotional upsets—you can nurture the baby, as well as prepare him or her to deal with the new environment after birth. Bonding with your baby sends a message that being loving is to be conscious of ways that can impact another human being as well as yourself.

♡ Heartfelt Points to Remember

♡ Physical well-being of the baby in utero starts with proper nutrition, exercise, and rest for the mother, to provide the best conditions for a child to thrive.

♡ Establish communication with the fetus to create a strong parental/child bond early on, by talking to the baby as much as possible.

♡ Create positive wishes/intentions for the baby that can be repeated often to affirm your dearest aspirations for the baby.

♡ Play soothing, relaxing music during pregnancy that will benefit both mother and baby.

♡ Resolve stress and upset emotional states during pregnancy so that stress hormones cannot affect the baby's nervous system and future emotional states.

♡ Communicate with the baby in utero to help establish a positive foundation for a loving parent/child relationship.

Bring on the Blue Chips

Who shall set a limit to the influence of a human being?

~RALPH WALDO EMERSON

Dear Aly,

Everyone told me that the first few months of motherhood were going to be overwhelming. Hearing those words was one thing, but experiencing them was completely different—and in some cases, "overwhelming" was an understatement! I had dealt with several stressful situations in my life, and I'd gotten through them without too much damage, so I figured I had this "handled" and could get through anything. I had already experienced the illness and death of your Grandpop Earl in my mid-twenties, separation and divorce from my first husband, and starting several new careers with their highly charged ups and downs.

I was naively confident that I was about to add parenthood to the list of the many challenges I had conquered. Was I ever wrong! It was a completely new experience for me. I felt humbled by my inexperience in taking care of a newborn and the knowledge that I had this huge responsibility for another human being. The first six weeks went by in a blur—they're still a blur even now! I was exhausted and more than a little bewildered. One night, I held you in my arms and wondered how I was going to make sure all my hopes and wishes for you would come true; and how I was going to fulfill my commitment to teaching you how to love yourself.

Maybe it was the powerful bond forming between us that etched this memory in my mind, but I can still remember that night and the thoughts that led me to begin my plan to teach you self-love. Just watching you, all giggles, smiles, and cooing when your dad and I held you, or when we walked into a room, I knew that children are born loving; they don't know any different. I had never heard of a baby born "hating"! It was as if you were born with a spark of love within the "package" that was you—all six and a half pounds and nineteen inches of you. It was my responsibility to keep that spark of love burning and never allow it to be extinguished, even when outside forces would try to chip away at it.

But how could I define what love really is? As poets have known for centuries, it's hard to come up with a definition of something so familiar and universal, so rather than try to define it I thought about the qualities that are the essence of love. One way to "remind" you of that loving spark every day was to make sure you were surrounded by loving people. Your dad and I possess loving qualities that I hoped you would imitate. But the truth is that loving people tend to express loving qualities: kindness, gentleness, loyalty, responsibility, acceptance, compassion, and respect, to name a few. Knowing that young children are like sponges and also that they tend to imitate those around them, I hoped that you would begin to absorb those loving qualities and model your behavior on the loving people in your life. So anytime I hired a babysitter, a nanny, or anyone that I thought would have an important influence in your life, I carefully observed them to be sure they possessed these loving qualities.

When I was looking at preschools for you, I was more interested in the qualities the teachers exhibited rather than their educational merits and degrees. Were they kind? Caring? Generous? Looking back now, I'm so grateful for the many loving people in your life. Your dad and I cocooned you with many caring people in addition to ourselves: a loving grandmother; many thoughtful and responsible babysitters; wonderful, accepting teachers; and our friends and close family relatives. You had many "mentors of love" in your life, and I'm so proud of the way you have taken small parts from each of these people and emulated them in your life. When I look at the now-completed puzzle of you, Aly, I can see individual pieces that were contributed by many of these wonderful people.

Love,
Mommy

*t*here is no doubt that in the first six months of a newborn's life a parent experiences a wide range of feelings: from trepidation, uneasiness, and being overwhelmed to joy and hope for the future and—of course—pure exhaustion! For new parents, especially those who had successful careers beforehand, the shock at how much they have to learn can be a humbling experience. Preparing and delivering solutions to difficult business problems seems mundane compared to figuring out an organizational strategy for an outing to the supermarket with a newborn! Even for second- or third-time parents, there is always a certain "amnesia" when it comes to remembering those exhausting first few months of newborn care.

Yet with all the early perils of infant childcare, even through the depths of exhaustion, all you have to do is simply look into the eyes of your newborn to see unconditional love. Infants radiate love. They are trusting and they don't pass judgment. They assume that they will automatically be loved and cared for, because the alternative is literally inconceivable to them.

Imagine, as an adult, that you felt totally safe in a warm place, that all your needs and wants were fulfilled, and then suddenly you were pushed out into a world where everything seemed strange and new and you became dependent upon complete strangers for survival. That is exactly what newborns go through. But even after enduring this ordeal, newborns begin their lives with openness and the ability to love. To them, it's not relevant if their parents are poor or rich, smart or illiterate; they love nonetheless. Babies come with the inherent wisdom that everyone deserves love, and that unconditional love comes naturally to them. Perhaps it is this innate sense that allows parents and other caregivers to fall in love with them so easily.

Love is often described as the universal language, yet with love's diverse meanings and all of the different interpretations of it, love is unusually difficult to define. Paramahansa Yogananda, author of the well-known book *Autobiography of a Yogi,* explains that "to describe love is very difficult, for the same reason that words cannot fully describe the flavor of an orange. You have to taste the fruit to know the flavor. So with love." So rather than trying to *define* love, think about the qualities that loving people possess or have in common. Kindness, acceptance, caring, compassion, respect, responsibility, honesty, affection, devotion, understanding, and patience are some of these. Then ask yourself if you would use any of these adjectives to describe yourself. Write down your own loving qualities and then put a star next to the ones that you would like your child to possess. Think of this as a "recipe" for self-love and you are listing some of the ingredients.

Awareness of your own loving qualities is important, since what we have within ourselves is usually what we desire in others. In this case, these qualities are the same ones that we hope others will use to describe our children or grandchildren someday. If you have described yourself as patient and accepting, then *live* these qualities.

Be patient and accepting around your children. Children first learn through imitation. Infants do not have the cognitive ability to knowingly discern the behaviors of their caregivers. They just end up "living" our actions and making them their own. Dr. Maria Montessori, the Italian educator who founded the Montessori educational movement said, "The child takes in his whole environment, not with his mind but with his life."

Research has established that imitation is a mechanism by which infants learn cause and effect. They are extremely observant of the effects their behaviors have on others. Since their survival depends on it, infants carefully observe which of their behaviors cause anger and which ones causes joy. Early learning also evolves from mimicry. The power of imitation plays an important role not only in infanthood but also in the first few years of childhood. Sometimes when children first learn something, they replay it over and over again like a broken record, and after the *thousandth* time, you may feel like you are losing it! But look at it this way: the brain needs repetition so that it can develop those pathways of learning. Rule of thumb: if you want your child to do something, do it first so that you can become a role model for them to imitate. Keep in mind those loving qualities that you bring to the table, the ones that you want them to "absorb" and imitate.

As your child grows beyond the newborn years, surround him or her with other people who also exhibit loving behaviors. Think of these people as your child's "blue chips." In financial circles, blue chip companies are known and accepted for their high quality. Look for blue chips when you interview babysitters, nannies, preschool teachers, or other adults that the child will spend time with (see the

Appendix on p. 115 for sample interview questions). The more people that behave lovingly around a child, the more opportunities for them to imitate and reinforce their natural tendency to love.

♡ **Love to Exercise 1** ♡

How do you identify your child's ideal blue chips? Take a moment and fill out the following form to help you identify those blue chip people and their loving qualities:

BLUE CHIPS
Identifying the People in Your Child's Life
Who Add Loving and Emotional Value

Use the lines below to write the loving qualities exhibited by the important people in your child's life.

Parents

Name: Loving Qualities:

_____

_____

Family

Name: Loving Qualities:

_____

_____

_____

_____

Teachers

Name: Loving Qualities:

_____

_____

_____

_____

Babysitters

Name: Loving Qualities:

_____

_____

_____

_____

♡ ♡ ♡

♡ Heartfelt Points to Remember

♡ Accept that the first few months of parenthood will overwhelm you at times and humble you at others.

♡ Infants are born loving: they radiate love. Simply look into a newborn's eyes to recognize this unconditional love.

♡ Identify the loving qualities that you believe you possess and the ones that you want for your child.

♡ Awareness of your own loving qualities is important, since what we have within ourselves is usually what we desire in others.

♡ The power of imitation plays an important role not only in infanthood but also in the first few years of childhood. If you want your child to imitate loving behavior, role model those loving qualities yourself.

♡ Identify and surround the child with as many "blue chips" as possible for imitation opportunities and to reinforce their natural tendency to love.

I Love Me . . .
Who Do You Love?

To love oneself is the beginning of a life-long romance.

~OSCAR WILDE

Dear Aly,

I never thought I would learn so much about myself by simply watching you grow up. As I experienced your progress from a happy, smiley infant into a willful, engaging toddler to an inquisitive and thoughtful five-year-old, there were times when all I saw was a "mini me." Sometimes when you spoke, I heard my own words coming out of your mouth and soon I began to notice that the expressions on your face matched mine. It was like looking in a mirror . . . a tiny reflection of me! Unfortunately, even the thoughts, beliefs, and behaviors that I didn't particularly like in myself were being transferred to you. This only reminded me what a huge responsibility it was to be your mother.

Parents often do things or act a certain way without consciously realizing it, and their actions often get replayed in our children through imitation. You know—monkey see-monkey do? I remember once when we were at the park, some children invited you to play with them in the sandbox. You refused to play with them no matter how many times they asked. You kept saying no. Crying, you told me, "I don't want my perfect dress to get dirty." It struck me that a three-and-a-half-year-old wouldn't know what those words meant unless they'd heard them before. And here I thought I was a "reformed" perfectionist! I had really worked hard on my perfectionist tendencies—only to find my own daughter struggling with the same trait. That day in the park made me realize that the most loving thing I could do as your mommy was to be aware, as best I could, of my own negative "hard-wired" thoughts, beliefs, and actions and to try to avoid having them become part of you.

I believed that I always had to be my parents' perfect little girl in order to get love from them. I carried that same belief into other relationships in my life as I grew up. It was as if I had to earn love to get love. I was so busy trying to win love that I was never able to embrace the love that I had within me. In figuring this out for myself, I realized that in order for me to help you learn self-love, I had to appreciate that the love you brought with you—your birthright—wasn't something you had to earn from me or anybody else; I just had to keep gently reminding you of your loving "spark."

One of the ways I "reminded" you of your own internal love was to use the pronoun "you" instead of "I" whenever I could, especially when I was praising you. When you'd ask, "Mommy, do you like my drawing?" instead of saying, "I love your drawing," I would turn it back to you and say, "Aly, do YOU like the drawing?" Invariably, you would reply with an enthusiastic "Yes!" at which point I would say, "Great, Aly, because YOU liking it is the important thing!" Then off you would go with a big smile on your face. When you got older and would come home from school telling me about a particular grade that you got on an exam, I would say, "Aly, YOU should be so proud of yourself! You studied really hard and that paid off in an A on the test. Good job!" I substituted the pronoun "you" whenever I could and as often as I could. Over and over again, I substituted "you" for "I" to create the message that your own accomplishments were not conditional on my approval nor my love. I wanted you to appreciate and love yourself for your own talents and accomplishments. This simple exercise, practiced over time, allowed you to internalize your achievements, and that boosted your own self-love, free of others' approval.

By the way, don't think I never said "I love you" or gave you praise. Both your dad and I did, but it was praise with meaning, not just empty words. We were very specific in the praise you received so you would know exactly what you were being praised for. We also used the words "I love you" along with loving actions, guiding and helping you better adapt to your environment. Hugs, kisses, and other affectionate gestures, as well as spending quality time interacting with you, let you know you were loved.

Sometimes, loving you meant helping you deal with things you were afraid of and finding ways for you to overcome them. As a toddler, you were afraid of going down high slides at the playground. Watching you cry at the top of the slide and knowing that your fear was stopping you from doing something you really wanted to do was not easy for me. I used loving actions and words of encouragement—and sometimes even went down those slides with you—to help you overcome your fear. Eventually, you became a slide champion! Helping you realize that this achievement was yours alone reinforced the love that you have for yourself.

My loving actions provided you with an emotional security blanket that allowed you to venture out and accomplish something on your own. You soon learned that one way of loving yourself was to do things to overcome the fears that stopped you from enjoying life. I believe that the greatest thing a parent can do to boost a child's self-esteem is to help them overcome a fear and turn it into a victorious achievement, not simply utter empty words of praise. Do you remember how you and I would often discuss your early slide victory (just one of many as you continued to grow)? I always made sure to speak of it in terms that reinforced your own loving talents. Loving yourself comes from the knowledge that your own accomplishments are based on you earning the ability to be courageous and to do things to your best ability. I just needed to remind of you of this as often as possible as you grew—and let you take all the credit.

Love,
Mommy

*M*ost parents enter parenthood with the intention of being the best parent they can be. We are like "investors" in our children's lives, committing to invest our time, energy, love, and guidance on a daily basis. As parents or caregivers, we also have to be cognizant of how dependent children are on us to guide them and help them learn how to get along in their environment. A child has to quickly learn so much information in order to survive and be a contributing part of his or her physical world.

The study of early brain activity provides clues as to how children are able to download this huge amount of information. In his book *The Biology of Belief*, Dr. Bruce Lipton discusses research regarding the brain's electrical activities as measured by electroencephalograms (EEGs). From birth to two years of age, children's brain waves mostly operate at the lowest EEG frequency—called delta waves (.05–4 Hz). Between the ages of two and six, a child's brain waves change from delta to a slightly higher frequency called theta (4–8 Hz). Interestingly, delta and theta frequencies are prominent in the practice of hypnotherapy. Hypnotherapists try to get their clients' brains to operate at lower frequencies because the brain is more suggestible when EEG frequencies are low (at delta and theta). This fact explains how young children absorb their parents' beliefs and attitudes directly into their subconscious mind, the part of the mind that is below awareness, that stores memory and organizes and processes experiences. Analogous to a computer and its hard drive with its stored bits and bytes, the programmable subconscious receives information from the child's environment that enables a parent's behavior and beliefs to become like the child's own. Young children do not have the cognitive ability to be discerning about the information they pick up from their parents and their environment and therefore they tend to accept that information as "truths" that end up shaping their behavior and approaches to life.

So what can parents do about this? It would be impossible for any parent to control the vast information their child absorbs and dictate how it will be interpreted and stored in their mind. However, the power of awareness plays an important role. We can only be responsible for changing things in our lives that we are conscious of. After personal examination, a parent may become aware of certain beliefs and attitudes that in the past have caused them difficulty in their lives. If so, they can make a conscious effort not to have those beliefs "transfer" to or influence their children. In my case, my perfectionist tendencies were picked up by my daughter without my awareness. Once I became aware that this behavior was being recycled in my child, I began to make a conscious effort to do something about it. What a tremendous gift we give our children by doing this. Why should they have to replicate our past experiences, disillusionments, and attitudes because of ill-suited beliefs? Look at parenthood as an excellent opportunity to try to change those old patterns.

♡ **Love to Exercise 2** ♡

To break a pattern of beliefs or attitudes, imagine that a genie has granted you the power to let go of at least three thoughts or beliefs about yourself that have caused you pain throughout the years. Was it about your body image or weight? How you performed academically in school and your perception of your intelligence? Perhaps it was a fearful, traumatic experience you went through. Whatever these beliefs or experiences may have been, write them down on a piece of paper or in a journal. Now take one of those old beliefs about yourself and imagine one of your children acting it out. With this new awareness, now visualize you giving your child a beautifully wrapped gift with a card inside explaining that you are giving her the gift of working on your own negative thoughts and experiences so that she won't have to repeat them.

Gift Card

My past negative thoughts, beliefs, and experiences are mine alone. This gift is my promise to work on them and not have them repeated in you. I love you.

With awareness and a commitment to break the chains of our past ill-suited beliefs, we allow our children to experience life through their own eyes—without our past weighing them down.

While we work on our own negative footprints and allow our children to determine and blaze their own trail, there are things we can do to remind them of that loving spark that is their birthright. As investors in a child's life, parents and caregivers can guide their child toward what I call *internal appreciation*. Internal appreciation is another way of explaining the self-love that is present when a person values and loves him/herself in a way that is not dependent upon others. It comes from knowing, on your own, that you are worthy, without outside validation. And just as a financial asset is said to appreciate when it grows in value, internal appreciation grows and matures over time. The beauty of internal appreciation is that it can keep on growing and expanding infinitely.

♡ Love to Exercise 3 ♡

A fun way to reinforce this concept of internal appreciation, especially in young children, and to remind them to love themselves, is what I call the "Love Hug."

Try this exercise yourself before sharing it with your child. Place your right hand on your left shoulder, then place your left hand on your right shoulder. Note that your right arm is right next to your heart. Holding your arms like this simulates a hugging sensation. With your eyes opened or closed, say the following out loud:

I love me,

I love thee,

I love myself in every way, every day!

How did doing this make you feel? Many people report a warm sensation flowing from the arms to the rest of the body. Do this exercise with your child every day. When they are infants, do it for them or let them watch you. Once they are able to talk, teach them how to do it. Make it a family ritual, either at night before they go to sleep or when they wake up in the morning.

Children are born without self-awareness. Only later, through inter-actions with other people, do children begin to develop their inter-nal sense of self. This growing awareness is part of the process of differentiating themselves from others and recognizing their own autonomy. To increase internal appreciation within a young child, redirect their external verification back to them. In the early years, children are always looking for ways to figure out who they are, especially based on their actions. One of the best ways to redirect their verification back toward them is to utilize what I call "Youer-Than-You" Statements. The name was taken from a book by my daughter's favorite author, Dr. Seuss:

> Today you are you,
> That is truer than true.
> There is no one alive
> Who is youer than you.

> —Dr. Seuss, *Oh, the Places You'll Go!*

It is normal for parents and caregivers to give children feedback based on their own perspective. Statements like "*I* really like that picture you drew" may be uttered without thinking. However, what the child actually hears in that "I" statement is the message that their action is conditional and based on *your* approval or disap-proval. Eventually, the child will always look *outside* of him/herself for approval instead of trusting his or her own internal validation. However, by simply changing the "I" to "You" when praising or being asked for feedback, the Youer-Than-You Statement helps encourage internal appreciation of a child's talents, self-image, and love for themselves.

Here are some examples of Youer-Than-You Statements:

1. A child asks for feedback on artwork or something that he or she has created.
    Child: Mommy/Daddy, do you like the finger painting I did?
    Parent: Do YOU like it?
    Child: Yes!
    Parent: Great, because YOU liking it is the most important thing!

2. A child tells you something wonderful that he or she accomplished or did during the day.
    Parent: YOU must be so (happy, excited, fortunate, pleased, delighted) that you _____ (fill in event or accomplishment).

3. A child tells you about a high mark he or she received on a test.
    Parent: "YOU must be so proud of that A. Studying hard for that test really paid off!"

4. A child asks you for specific feedback on how he/she did on a particular activity (for example, performing a song).
    Parent: "YOU sang that song so well. YOU sang each verse slowly and clearly. YOU also clapped your hands with each verse! It sounded great!"

Always starting praise with "you" might take a little getting used to, but over time, it will begin to feel natural and will become automatic. Praising your child in this way creates a powerful subconscious signal that ignites your child's inner loving spark. More importantly, it also encourages them to look within themselves for acknowledgment of their own gifts and talents, building confidence, and security. Imagine if all your life you had been constantly given compliments or had others always giving you feedback or praise about yourself or actions, and then suddenly the source of those compliments was no longer available? Then what? What we want to create in the formative years of a young child's life is the assurance that they won't have to depend on others for constant validation. Self-love or internal appreciation takes care of that automatically.

So, does using "you" mean that you never use the first person "I" when talking to your child? Of course not! When we praise or give feedback to our children, it is important to be cognizant of the fact that being specific and inner-directed as opposed to outer-directed is in the child's best interest. There is a presumption that the more we give our children praise—like telling them how smart, beautiful, or wonderful they are—the more they will come to believe it and, thus, become that way.

Research shows, however, that quite the opposite is true. In the book *NatureShock,* by Po Bronson and Ashley Merryman, the authors present research by Dr. Carol Dweck, who studied the effects of praise on students in twenty New York schools. In their study of intelligence and performance, Dr. Dweck and her team of researchers found that "generic" praise—"You are so smart"— backfired when children experienced difficulty or challenges. The children who had been repeatedly told they were smart were so concerned with living up to that title that they would often simply give up if something was too difficult for them rather than risk failure. However, when praise was specific to the accomplishment, so that a child knew exactly what they did to deserve the praise—"You did well on that math test because you studied and learned those multiplication tables"—they performed better on tests. They also appeared to be more motivated and less risk-averse in finding ways that would overcome any challenges that stood in their way. Psychologists Jennifer Henderlong Corpus and Mark Lepper performed an analysis of thirty years of studies on the effects of praise and found that praise can be a powerful force with children if it is sincere and specific; contains realistic, attainable goals for accomplishment; and focuses on mastery of skills verses comparison to others.

How did we as parents get so addicted to praise? Perhaps it began back in the 1970s and 1980s with the huge self-esteem movement that propagated the idea that in order to improve and create a positive sense of self for children, all one needed to do was give them positive praise regardless of whether it was true or not. During that era, it was sacrilegious for teachers and parents to criticize or negatively comment on a child's performance. Positive praise flowed like beer at a fraternity party! Another reason excessive praise has become commonplace is that, without realizing it, as parents we somehow equate praise with unconditional love. Directing high levels of praise toward our children made us feel better about our roles as parents. Perhaps the underlying reason, truth be told, is that parents believed that if we told them how proud we were of them or how great they are, it would assuage our anxieties about our own parenting skills.

Yet praise, when used correctly, *can* be an effective tool for building a child's internal appreciation. In order to do so, it must be specific and inner-directed. It must be intentional, with meaning. Children are very astute and can sniff out praise with no truth behind it. It's the same thing as saying "I love you" to children. Babies hear those words, but they don't cognitively understand their meaning; yet they can sense or feel something special. The tone of the voice, the smile, the tender touch is what they pick up on. These cues translate into a connection, which creates a blanket of security in which the child feels that they are being taken care of. Survival in their physical environment depends on this security. Telling your child that you love him is indeed important, as long as it is said with meaning. And, more importantly, loving actions speak louder than any words. The energy behind those loving actions is like a boomerang of love back to the child that can guide him or her in overcoming fears and becoming more confident.

Watching your child struggle with something they cannot do or fear of trying something new is difficult for most parents. Often, because of our love for them, we want to rush in and "fix" the situation for them, protecting them from failure. Yet the most loving thing to do in almost every case is to help them overcome their fears with proper support. Helping them tune into their own internal appreciation for themselves by conquering a fear of something becomes a powerful motivating force for learning how to overcome other obstacles in life. I was able to help my daughter get over her fear of going down the slide by lovingly supporting her, and that achievement provided a tremendous standing ovation for her sense of self and strong reinforcement of her internal appreciation.

To continue to prime the pump and increase a child's internal appreciation, that love spark, for themselves, make sure that for every "I love you" there is an equal amount of "I love me." Telling our children that we love them doesn't necessarily translate into them learning to love themselves. True, it sounds nice and it does provide a feeling of security for them, which, as mentioned earlier, is important. As investors in our children's lives, our real work is to remind them of the internal love with which they were born. The love is already there, like a reservoir waiting to be utilized. Help your child tap into their reservoir of self-love through appropriate praise along with Youer-Than-You Statements. Use the Love Hug often with your children—and don't forget to use it yourself. Trust me, there's nothing better than getting a hug, especially from oneself!

♡Heartfelt Points to Remember

♡ Children's brain activity from birth to six years of age allows them to absorb and download information, behaviors, and beliefs from others that end up shaping their behavior and approach to life.

♡ By making an inventory of your own beliefs and attitudes that in the past have caused difficulty for you, you can make a conscious effort to avoid having them "transfer" to or unduly influence your children.

♡ Internal appreciation is when a person values and loves himself or herself and that love is not conditional on actions or praise from others. Practice the Love Hug often to reinforce a child's internal appreciation.

♡ Use Youer-Than-You Statements to direct external verification back toward your child, increasing internal appreciation or self-love.

♡ When using praise, make it specific and inner-directed rather than vague and external.

♡ Be intentional and meaningful when saying "I love you" to a child, and back it up with loving actions.

Instilling
Empathetic
Acceptance

I Am Who I Am . . .
And You Ain't Gonna Change Me

The principle of all successful effort is to try to do not what is absolutely the best, but what is easily within our power, and suited for our temperament and condition.

~John Ruskin

Dear Aly,

People often ask me if you were always the same happy, smiling person that you are today. The answer is, yes, you were exactly like that from day one. The idea of a baby coming into the world with an entire set of traits untainted by anyone's influence always fascinated me. I once asked my mom (Nanny) to describe what my brother, my sister, and I were like when we were babies. She told me, "I remember asking the pediatrician why your brother, Gary, seemed so intense and angry. Nothing I did seemed to calm him. The pediatrician told me that was just the way he was born, and it didn't matter what I did. You were the complete opposite: easygoing and very complacent. Five and a half years later, when your sister Jane was born, she was colicky at first, so she cried a lot, but after the first few months she calmed down and settled into a personality that was a combination of you and your brother. Not as intense as Gary, but not as easygoing as you were." It's funny: those descriptions still hold true of the three of us; knowing your aunt and uncle, I'm sure you'd agree!

What Nanny was really describing is what is called temperament. Simply defined, temperament is a set of traits you are born with that remain with you as you grow to adulthood and that determine how you interact with and react to the world around you. It's like your behavioral style—it's not what you do, but how you do it. You are probably more familiar with the more common term "personality." But personality is actually the combination of temperament and the life experiences that shape and influence one's development and behavior. That sweet, loving way that so many people notice and continue to comment about you, to this day, is the nature you were born with it. Was I ever blessed!

Knowing you, you probably want to know how I would describe you using those temperament traits, right? Well, here goes—As a psychologist, I would describe you in the following way: average activity level; not easily distracted by outside influences; medium intensity level for how you respond to people emotionally; regular in terms of how your own internal biological clock regulates sleep and appetite; high sensory threshold, especially to sounds, taste, and touch; a cautious approach in how you respond to new people and situations; an average adaptability level to changes and transitions; fairly persistent in terms of working through difficult activities; and a positive mood in the way you react to the world. Now here's the "Mommy-ese" version: You always woke up happy, and nine times out of ten you went to bed the same way. You were easygoing and got along well with friends. You didn't like loud voices and noises, especially if someone yelled at you; you were hesitant and cautious with new situations until you got used to the transition—then you would be off as if it was nothing new; you would never give up until you accomplished difficult tasks—not that you didn't struggle sometimes. Finally, I loved how you always kept smiling and stayed optimistic, even in the face of challenging situations. I'm sure when you think about it yourself, you will agree with this description, since it's how teachers and other significant people in your life described you again and again over the last eighteen years. It's just who you are, and that's never going to change.

But how does your temperament relate to my commitment to you—teaching you self-love? Well, first I had to understand how your temperament traits combine to make you this very special person. By being able to understand your uniqueness, I learned to respect, honor, and accept you for who you are. My acceptance of you and all of your strengths and frailties allowed you to begin to become accepting of yourself. Self-acceptance is a very important component of self-love.

And Aly, watching you accept yourself so completely helped me learn to better accept myself. If I could value you for all of your talents and weaknesses, why couldn't I do the same for me? It occurred to me that up until this point in my own life, I was still critical of what I perceived as my shortcomings. I had to learn to stop criticizing what was wrong with me in order to be kind to myself. But a tape in my head kept repeating thoughts that I was "never good enough." The moment I started to see myself accepting you, I could better accept myself for who I was, and my inner critic stopped beating me up. My role in your life was to remind you of that "inner spark of love" within, but I discovered that I needed to remind myself as well. I began to tap into that reservoir of self-love, and that made me feel worthy of love and gave me a sense of fulfillment and greater freedom to express myself. Who knew my journey with you would become my own?

When you started school full time at age five, you were surrounded by many different children from a variety of backgrounds and experiences. You liked to wear dresses when other girls liked pants, and your athletic ability was a far cry from your soccer playing, jump roping, and dodgeball playing friends. I had to accept your "girliness," so unfamiliar to me given my former tomboy status. Your stubborn refusal to wear the colorful overalls I bought you taught me to honor your desire to wear twirly dresses and dress up your Barbie dolls. And, no, you didn't have the athletic abilities like your father, but we proudly accepted and respected your artistic endeavors. When you saw us accepting and appreciating you for the qualities that you brought to the world, it sent the message that you could accept and love yourself, too.

Love,
Mommy

*W*hen we become parents, our children's uniqueness often surprises us. Sue, a mother of four, describes each of her children in this way: "Johnny, the oldest, is my happiest, most easygoing child out of the four. He wakes up happy and can handle change of routine pretty easily as he just rolls with the punches. Now, Debbie, my middle child, is the complete opposite! She gets upset easily, and I could never get her to be on a regular schedule for sleeping or eating. Anything can set her off emotionally, and she gets very cranky if there is a change in her routine. After Debbie, Sam was almost a relief! He's the shyest out of the four and often more of an observer than an active participant. He's my bookworm, and he prefers doing quiet activities like puzzles and art projects. Our youngest, Jake, seems to be constantly on the move. He's the one who—I swear—ran before he even walked and whose energy level could light up a house! My husband and I can't believe we have four such completely different children!"

Many of the characteristics Sue describes in her four children relate to inborn *temperament,* identified by researchers Alexander Thomas and Stella Chess after a long-term longitudinal study in the 1950s. Temperament refers to the genetic traits that determine how an individual will interact with his or her environment. It is a component of one's personality, which combines both the genetically determined traits and the thoughts, feelings, behaviors, and experiences that make each person unique. Thomas and Chess's New York Longitudinal Study, which started in 1956 and continued over several decades, followed 136 children into adulthood and identified nine characteristics or traits associated with temperament:

1. Activity level (extent of motor activity)

2. Adaptability (transitions or changes in the environment)

3. Approach/Withdrawal (willingness to approach or withdraw from people, objects, or experiences)

4. Persistence (tolerance for frustration and span of attention in an activity)

5. Intensity (positive or negative response to emotions or responses)

6. Distractibility (level of distraction from outside influences)

7. Mood (predominant disposition both positive or negative determining reaction to the world)

8. Regularity (the internal biological clock for eating, elimination, and sleeping)

9. Sensory threshold (sensitivity to external stimuli like sound, taste, touch, and temperature)

Chess and Thomas recognized that some of the temperament traits overlapped in children, so they consolidated the groupings into three types: the easy child, the difficult child, and the slow-to-warm child. Eventually other researchers added another category: the active child. These four temperament styles are usually apparent very early in life, typically by four months of age. Keep in mind that the four categories are just average profiles and that in reality children's personalities are a unique blend of the nine traits as well as other life experiences.

♡ Love to Exercise 4 ♡

To help you identify the temperament of your baby or child, look over the descriptions of the four temperament groupings. As you read each one, check off which one best describes your child. Remember, one category is in no way better than the other—no judgment! Also, children can be a mixture of some of the categories.

1. The Easy Child:
   - ☐ Wakes up happy
   - ☐ Eating and sleeping are pretty regular
   - ☐ Easily adapts to new situations, considered "easygoing"
   - ☐ Open to new experiences and enjoyable to be around
   - ☐ Moderate in expression of emotions

2. The Difficult Child:
   - ☐ Easily upset and difficult to console
   - ☐ Irregular in eating and sleeping patterns
   - ☐ Reacts irritably to change of routine
   - ☐ Emotionally intense

3. The Slow-to-Warm Child:
   - ☐ Needs time to adjust to transitions and changes

☐ More of an observer than a participant

☐ Lower level of intensity

☐ More cautious and prefers quieter play activities

4. The Active Child:

☐ Difficulty with self-control and impulsivity

☐ Seems to be always in motion; rather run than walk, climb any obstacle, and leap before they look

☐ Very high energy level

♡ ♡ ♡

A child's temperament is part of his unique personality. He couldn't change it even if he wanted to. As a parent or caregiver, rather than fight to change your child's temperament, study it. Look at these temperament traits as your child's assets. In the financial world, assets are the total value of everything a corporation or business owns. A child comes into this world "owning" what she or he is, and as investors in our children's lives, it's important to recognize, accept, and value your child for who they truly are.

Sometimes, when there are inherent differences between the temperaments of parent and child, parents tend to have a harder time accepting children and will try all kinds of things to change them. This sets up a difficult interplay between you and your child that will only lead to friction and unhappiness. I grew up as a tomboy, and having a feminine girl who only wanted to wear frilly dresses and play with dolls was something I had difficulty relating to. At first, I tried to convince her to wear overalls and play sports, but the more I pushed her, the more she resisted. Her resistance caused tension between us, which made me feel uncomfortable. Even though she did not share my temperament traits, I continued to see myself as the template I thought she should follow. I finally realized that I was judging her instead of accepting who she really was. I realized that acceptance is also part of loving oneself. What message was I sending her if I didn't accept her with all of her talents and weaknesses? However, I came to realize that if I modeled acceptance of her, then she, in turn, could learn self-acceptance.

One of the key components of loving oneself is accepting all aspects of your being, what I call *empathetic acceptance,* which is the ability to perceive one's own feelings, talents, strengths, and weaknesses with full understanding, compassion, and tolerance. Part of teaching children how to love themselves is enabling them to have empathetic acceptance. To best understand their perspective, ask yourself the question, "How accepting am I of my own faults and weaknesses?" Does your inner critic immediately jump in and tick off your failures and mistakes? As I was learning to accept Aly for who she was, I realized that I, too, needed to accept my own perceived shortcomings. What helped me the most in accomplishing this was a good dose of kindness toward myself. Being kind to myself meant turning off my inner critic and realizing that empathetic acceptance starts with appreciating all of me, warts and all! As I undertook this transformation, I found that I was much more able to project this understanding and acceptance onto my daughter. It's like lighting a candle: what shines within you, illuminates others.

♡Heartfelt Points to Remember

♡ Temperament refers to the genetic traits that dictate how an individual will interact with their environment.

♡ A person's temperament is part of his or her unique personality. Even if you want to change it, you cannot.

♡ Nine temperament traits make up our innate blueprint.

♡ The four temperament categories, or "profiles," for children are: the easy child, the difficult child, the slow-to-warm child, and the active child.

♡ It's important to recognize, accept, and value your child's traits and personality, the things that make them who they truly are.

♡ Empathetic acceptance is the ability to perceive one's own feelings, talents, strengths, and weaknesses with full understanding, compassion, and tolerance.

♡ Learn to embrace your own empathetic acceptance to pave the way for your child to do the same—leading to self-love.

To Be or Not to Be . . .
That Is the Question

The fruit of self-understanding is self-acceptance. The fruit of self-acceptance is self-love. The fruit of self-love is love for the world. The fruit of love for the world is service to the world. The fruit of service to the world is peace.

~RUSSELL ROWE

Dear Aly,

When you were little, Daddy and I were your greatest influences. When you went to elementary school, your friends, peers, and teachers became your primary influences. As we grow up and expand our horizons, we get many messages about ourselves from the outside world, and these messages contribute to our own opinions about how we are supposed to act, look, or even think. That's why I knew your elementary school years were an important time for creating a strong foundation of self-acceptance, or what I call empathetic acceptance, that you could continue to build upon. I believe that this is a key piece in the puzzle of learning self-love.

Do you remember the times you came home from school really upset and would tearfully tell me about something mean your friends had said or done? Usually your first reaction was indignation, like: "I can't believe they could say that to me!" Sometimes you even believed the mean-spirited things they said about you were true. After I wiped your tears and let you vent your anger and hurt feelings, we would talk about why your friends' mean comments bothered you so much. Usually what really bothered you was that what was said touched upon something you didn't like or questioned about yourself. Maybe you believed you weren't as physically coordinated on the monkey bars as some of your friends were, or you couldn't do math problems as quickly as some of your classmates. When other kids teased you, it felt like they had exposed those "deep, dark secrets" that you held inside about your weaknesses. And nobody likes to think others can see those limitations or imperfections that we think about ourselves!

So here's the deal, Aly—when we are self-accepting, we are able to embrace all facets of ourselves, not just the positive parts. It means that it is unconditional and free of qualifications. In particular, when we recognize and accept all of our weaknesses and limitations, this awareness will not interfere with our ability to fully accept ourselves and love every aspect of who we are. When we learn to accept what I used to call your "secret shadow" self, which includes your weaknesses and those critical thoughts about yourself, we can finally learn to see ourselves as a whole being—the good, the bad, and the ugly. After all, we are not perfect. That's why I always let you express your feelings and thoughts without judgment. The more we push away and bury those perceived unacceptable thoughts, feelings, and behaviors, the more secretive they become. Then you must work very hard to make sure nobody finds out about your "secret shadow" self. You'll recognize it when you see friends brag about themselves so that other people won't catch on to their flaws or when you see traits or behaviors in other people that you don't like or that make you angry and realize that you actually share these traits. The truth of the matter, Aly, is that when we don't deal with or embrace our shadow self, it has a way of showing up when we least expect it.

Let me share an experience that really helped me understand the whole concept of this shadowy, secret self. Like you, I was always a good student who took academics seriously. I couldn't breeze through school and still do well, though; I had to work for my grades. Somewhere along the way, I believed that the fact that getting good grades took such hard work on my part meant that I wasn't smart enough. This notion was my "secret shadow" self. I worked very hard to make sure people wouldn't find out. I took difficult classes in college to prove to others that I could compete in a top academic arena, and I would read many magazines or journals so that I could keep up with current events and sound "well-informed" and smart. Many years later, when I was in graduate school and working on my senior research project, I worked with a select committee of top professors who would ultimately decide whether I earned my degree. My research project was the last piece of the requirements necessary to pass if I were to receive my graduate degree. Each time I met with this committee, I found myself becoming increasingly anxious. Even though I had a high grade point average and had passed my written and oral exams, underneath it all, I worried that they would find out my "secret." One day I was reading one of those magazine surveys where you ask your spouse to name three things that they really admire about you. When I asked Daddy to name three things that he admired about me he said, "I like that you are really smart, you are compassionate, and you have a very loving nature." I'm not sure why his comments made such an impression on me, but I suddenly realized that I must be the only one who thought I wasn't smart! I realized that the "secret" that I wasn't smart enough simply wasn't true, and I felt as if a huge weight had been lifted from me. I no longer felt anxiety about my research committee and getting my degree. I realized that I could not possibly know everything (my own definition of smartness), and that by accepting that, I could love my "unsmartness." By loving the parts of me that I saw as weaknesses, I could now embrace and make peace with them, since accepting every aspect of myself put me on the path toward self-love.

Do you remember in first grade, you had a dark-haired friend who made fun of your blonde hair, calling it "yellow"? I'll never forget your comment back to her. You told her that you loved your "yellow" hair because it was a part of you. I was so happy—you were getting it! When you love all aspects of yourself—yellow hair and all!—comments others make will not allow you to question if you are "okay" or "good enough," you already know you are! Being able to simply affirm that we are who we are, free of judgment, with whatever strengths or weaknesses we possess, we cannot help but be accepting. Accepting yourself allows you to be accepting of other people's differences. What a different world we would live in if this one lesson could be taught and learned worldwide!

Love,
Mommy

When we let go of our children's hands on the first day of school, it marks an important transition. For the first time, they will be influenced by people other than their parents. During a child's school years, his or her circle of influence widens to include the opinions and beliefs of teachers, peers, and other adults, who provide feedback regarding their physical appearance, academic standing, social status, and athletic abilities. These messages help shape how children come to see their own strengths and weaknesses. Because of this, the school years are important in instilling empathetic acceptance, a key ingredient in the recipe for self-love.

What does *empathetic acceptance* really mean? It is different from self-esteem, which refers to how we value what we consider our worthwhile attributes. As discussed in Chapter 4, empathetic acceptance is more inclusive since it embraces *all* facets of ourselves, not just the positive parts. Being aware of our weaknesses and limitations allows us to see a complete picture of ourselves, not just an "edited" version. Let us not confuse it with self-improvement, in which we keep trying to "fix" ourselves, aiming for the crowned achievement of perfection. Empathetic acceptance is avowing—without judgment—that we are who we are, in that moment, with all of our attributes and faults.

Whether you are a new parent or a seasoned one with several children, there will be times when your child will come home from school or from some extracurricular activity complaining that some friend or friends said something derogatory about them. Just like my daughter Aly, whose classmates made fun of her "yellow" hair or her lack of athletic ability on the playground, our children need our help in dealing with the parts of themselves that they have deemed unacceptable. As a parent, I have always wondered how children pick up these "not-good-enough" messages. But as a psychologist, I understand how these messages are interpreted differently from what parents might have originally intended.

Even children who are born into loving households can have overly sensitive "antennae" that pick up both the negative and positive feelings that are intermingled with their parents' love. Added to the mix are messages that we transmit to our children about whether their behavior is acceptable or unacceptable and the fact that we may dole out our love based on that. So when children identify behaviors they perceive as objectionable or unacceptable, they in turn come to see themselves as unacceptable. Somehow all of this can be interpreted, in unspoken terms, as: "I'm selfish and I'm not attractive enough, smart enough, thin enough, or good enough, and because of this, I must be unacceptable. Who could ever love me?"

What causes these feelings of unacceptability that arise from the human psyche? A child is born with an innate expectation that all of its physical and emotional needs will be met. As any parent knows, this is an impossible expectation. But a child does not know this, and when they begin to feel that their needs are not being met, they may internalize this as being unworthy of their parents' love. They wonder what's wrong with them that causes Mommy and Daddy to not love them, and they wonder what they have to do to earn back that love. If, after reading this, you feel overwhelmed and worried that you have created a pattern of unacceptance in your child and that you have somehow failed him, don't despair! The truth is that it's not anyone's fault and that being human means that we all have human failings. Unfortunately, we have not evolved enough as a species to be born with the instinctual ability to correctly decipher all the different messages that get misinterpreted when we are young. The good news is that our brains are always learning new adaptations and can replace old beliefs and thinking patterns that no longer serve us well. Helping a child learn empathetic acceptance is one of those adaptations.

♡ Love to Exercise 5 ♡

To help children learn empathetic acceptance, we must begin by helping them identify *all* the different aspects of themselves, including the parts of them that they perceive as undesirable or as their weaknesses. The goal is for them to understand that all of these apects of themselves are like a jigsaw puzzle, and the puzzle is not complete unless all the pieces are put together to make a whole.

Before you begin this exercise, it is important to first explain that everyone has things that they really like about themselves and other things that they would rather keep secret (so that nobody finds out about their weaknesses). Under the positive heart column, write in those aspects that your child

all of me puzzle

_____   _____

_____   _____

_____   _____

_____   _____

sees as his strengths, and in the negative heart column, write your child's perceived notions about his secret weaknesses. Since it may be difficult for your child to verbalize her weaknesses, or she may be reluctant to allow you to hear them, it might be easier if you first set an example by completing the

"All of Me Puzzle" for yourself. It may help your child to see that even parents and other adults are an imperfect mixture of both strengths and weaknesses. Once you have completed all the "puzzle pieces" for your child, explain that the whole puzzle makes up who she is in the moment now. By accepting all aspects of themselves, and especially by allowing those "secret" shadow parts of themselves to be known, children can learn to love and accept all the facets of who they are.

Does this mean that children and adults can never change aspects of their personality or improve themselves? No, but it depends on how one chooses to make these changes. Making changes, whether it is to your external appearance or to a particular aspect of your behavior, is easier when you are choosing to do it from an accepting, loving place rather than from a hateful or shameful position. For example, "I love my brunette hair, but I now choose to become a blonde so that I can experience what a different hair color looks like on me," is a more loving statement than "I hate my dark hair! If I'm blonde, I'll get more attention and I'll like myself better!" Note that in the first statement, there was full acceptance about being a brunette, with no judgment that having darker hair was better or worse than being a blonde. Compare this with the second statement, which contains harsh judgment about hair color causing unhappiness. Coloring one's hair may make someone feel more likeable or nicer-looking, but changing it only changes the hair, not any negative feelings about it.

Applying empathetic acceptance in our lives is also about living in the moment and not being future oriented. This means that a child is already okay and feels "good enough" about himself now. He does not focus on living his life in the future, thinking, "I'll be really liked *when* I win the baseball championship," or "*As soon as* I get straight As in all of my classes, I'll know that I'm really smart." When one achieves empathetic acceptance, there are no qualifications regarding our frailties. We accept ourselves now as who we are.

♡ Love to Exercise 6 ♡

This is a powerful exercise to help your child practice empathetic acceptance in the moment. Have your child stand in front of a mirror. Ask them to take a few moments to look in the mirror and then describe to you what they see in their reflection. For

example, "I see me smiling with two teeth missing. I have brown hair and blue eyes. I have tomato sauce on my shirt, and I'm wearing a blue skirt." After describing to you what they see in the mirror, have them place their hands, palms together, in front of them and repeat out loud: **"I accept myself, in this moment, just the way I am."** You may want to have them say this a few times. Have them do this mirror exercise in the morning, or before or after bath time. Mirror exercises are powerful, because the mirror reflects images to the brain through the eyes as if another person is actually looking at and speaking to you.

Just as parents need to accept and honor the innate blueprint of temperament that children bring into the world with them, so, too, do children need to apply the principle of empathetic acceptance in their lives. As children form friendships and relationships outside the family, they begin to deal with the social issues of peer pressure and bullying, along with trying to fulfill societal norms and expectations for appearance and behavior. When a child can fully accept all of his strengths and weaknesses, this allows him to truthfully understand his place in the world and to be comfortable with the knowledge of who he is. We can add to the old adage "Sticks and stones may break my bones, but words will never hurt me" the idea that our own critical, negative thoughts about who we are have no power over us when we can accept and love ourselves.

♡ Heartfelt Points to Remember

♡ Empathetic acceptance is more inclusive than self-esteem, since it embraces *all* facets of ourselves, not just the positive parts.

♡ Empathetic acceptance is about being non-judgmental with all of our attributes and faults.

♡ Children's feelings of unacceptability stem from their innate expectation that all their needs will be met by adults. When this unrealistic expectation that their needs are not met, they sometimes incorrectly come to the conclusion that this is somehow their "fault."

♡ Learn to recognize, understand, and accept the "secret shadow" self.

♡ Making changes within yourself is easiest when you choose to make changes from an accepting, loving place rather than from a hateful or shameful position.

♡ Practice empathetic acceptance in the moment and do not be future oriented.

Embracing Truth
or Consequences

If I Think It,
It Must Be True (lol)

Change your thoughts, and you change your world.

~Norman Vincent Peale

Dear Aly,

Back in the 60s and 70s, the "olden" days, there was a popular game show on TV called Truth or Consequences. In the game, if you couldn't answer a trivia question—the "Truth" portion—there would be "Consequences," usually some wacky stunt you had to perform. But sometimes the consequences consisted of a wonderful surprise for the contestant such as estranged or long-separated people being reunited. Those episodes always brought me to tears—you know what a sucker I am for a happy ending. The host always signed off with, "Hoping all your consequences are happy ones!" I loved hearing that consequences could be happy.

When I was your age, I thought being loved was like the name of that game show: if you were a "good girl" (truth), you earned love, attention and praise, and if you weren't, you would suffer rejection or alienation (consequences). I don't believe my parents, who were loving, wonderful people, meant for me to see love that way, but I did. Now that I am an adult, I view loving myself so differently, and I can see the meaning of "truth" or "consequences" in relation to loving yourself in a different light.

When it came to you loving yourself, I wanted to create a different path of truth than the one that I grew up with. One of the "truths" was learning how to deal with your thoughts. Especially as a teenager, I know your head is full of so many conflicting thoughts that it must be so confusing for you. You may not realize it—or maybe you do—but your mind is constantly creating thousands of thoughts every day. They come and go so quickly that most of the time you can't even distinguish when one ends and the other begins. Unfortunately many of our thoughts fall into the "negative" and "not true" categories. For example, when you drop a pencil on the floor during class, you might think, "Ugh, I can't believe I dropped that stupid pencil. Darn, now I have to pick it up!" (negative). Or let's say you are walking to class and you see two of your friends talking, and one just happens to glance your way. True or not, your mind goes to, "Oh, no . . . they must be talking about me since they didn't invite me over! Don't they like me?" (not true). Do any of those thoughts sound familiar? Or what about not even thinking someone else is thinking badly of you but you thinking bad thoughts about yourself? Thoughts like: "My nose is too big," "My hair is too curly and frizzy," or "I can't join because I am not good enough." Allowing critical thoughts like these to occupy space in your head is like beating yourself up over and over again. When you self-criticize, you believe and, in many cases, convince yourself that you are not okay. The sad part about this is that when you believe these critical thoughts, you convince yourself that you are not worthy of love. And then, instead of looking toward yourself, you look for compliments from others to vali-date and convince yourself that those things are not true. My goodness, we are all so hard on ourselves and in most cases so kind to others . . . does something seem wrong with this picture? I think so, and I certainly did not want this for you!

To help you with this, one of the strategies I taught you was to ask two very simple questions: "Is this thought really true? If so, how do I know that for sure?" When I did this, the first thing you did was think about those questions. When you really took the time to question the truth of your thoughts, your brain switched to deductive thinking, in which it began to analyze that question and "dissect" that original thought, attempting to find evidence to support or refute it. Oh, how the mind toys with us, Aly! The funny thing about it is that when we think a thought, we tend to believe that it must be true. And that is definitely not true! The reality is that 80 percent of our daily thoughts aren't true. Another thing that our brains do really well is coming up with "convinc-

ing evidence" to support our thoughts. It's like a lawyer is in our heads defending the case to the jury or judge—only instead of "innocent until proven guilty," our negative thoughts are "true until proven false." It is so sad that the pain we often feel is really the result of non-true thoughts that we inflict on ourselves. The good news is that we can change those thoughts by ruling out the false ones.

Remember how you felt after learning to question thoughts that gave you butterflies in your stomach? When you realized those thoughts were not true, you felt calm and much more peaceful. Your smile returned, and you knew that you could find a "truer thought" to replace the false one.

The truth is that when you create untrue thoughts that criticize yourself or put yourself down, you are not respecting that "inner spark" within. Remember, that spark is your birthright; it is just like a piece of silver jewelry that needs to be kept polished. When you were younger, it was my role to remind you of this and to do what I could to nurture it. Now that you are older and capable of doing this for yourself, you need to realize that you have the power to stop critical, non-loving, and untrue thoughts by questioning them. In so doing, you also get to remind yourself of the gentle, everlasting reservoir of unlimited love, compassion, and acceptance you are entitled to.

Love,
Mommy

OUR THOUGHTS HAVE MUCH TO do with the concept of self-love. Our brains manufacture thousands of thoughts a day. In fact, according to Daniel Amen, psychiatrist and author of the best-selling book *Change Your Brain, Change Your Life,* our brains produce sixty thousand thoughts a day. That's a lot of thoughts! Dr. Amen has also found that our overall state of mind depends upon the types of thoughts we think. When we activate a part of our brain that largely has to do with our emotional memories, and mix in fear and anxiety, our mind's lens focuses primarily on what Amen calls *automatic negative thoughts,* or ANTs. Examples of childhood and teen ANTs are:

- "Nobody in my class likes me."

- "I can't do this."

- "I never get picked to help the teacher."

- "No boy will ever like me because I'm not pretty enough."

- "I didn't do well on my test because I'm not smart."

- "I'll never get into a good college because there are much better students than me applying."

These thoughts and others like them are hopeless, judgmental, critical, and doubting and seem to bubble up without our permission. Unfortunately, while we may not realize it, the majority of our thoughts are of this type, and we tend to believe that if we think a thought it must be true. And because thoughts are a normal process of the mind, we must make an effort to observe these automatic thought processes (especially those ANTs) and to recognize that the persistent, negative inner statements are not true. Most thoughts are just ideas that we come to believe, but they can impact us in the ways we feel and behave, which can have huge consequences. Persistent thoughts eventually become habitual, and then they form a belief structure. This belief structure can shape the way we live our lives, positively or negatively. The truth is that these thoughts or beliefs are not hurtful or harmful unless we get attached to them. We get attached to our thoughts when we believe they are true without questioning them. Unfortunately, there isn't a school or any kind of formal place where we're taught to challenge these persistent thoughts. The good news is that we can learn to change these habitual negative thought processes by simply questioning them before they can produce painful, unloving repercussions.

♡ **Love to Exercise 7** ♡

To help a child or teen learn to question the thoughts that cause them stress or emotional pain, I use a technique called the *Thought Lie Detector Approach*. Just like the test that the police use to determine if someone is telling the truth, we can use this simple but powerful strategy to help our children decipher the "truth" in their thoughts, thoughts that may seem real and true but are actually destructive and causing them to be unhappy.

STEP ONE: We need to help children learn to "catch" thoughts that cause stress or discomfort. Statements that have the word "should" in them are prime candidates. "I should have been nicer to Sally and now she hates me!" "I should do better in school," "I shouldn't eat that cookie because I'll get fat." Another way to "catch" a thought causing children stress is to help them become aware of the feeling right before the thought. If the child can't describe or name the feeling, ask her where in her body she feels it. It could feel like a lump in the throat or butterflies in the stomach. Ask her: "If that place in the body where you feel something could talk, what would it say?" Feelings are similar to the smoke signals that the Native Americans used to convey the message that the enemy was coming. Feelings of fear are an especially strong indicator that related thoughts are not true.

STEP TWO: Ask the question, "Is this thought *really* true?" If the answer is "yes," ask the next question: "If so, how do you know for sure?" Ask for evidence. Usually, the evidence is simply other thoughts that seem to support and justify the thought.

STEP THREE: As untrue thoughts begin to unravel and show their "untruthfulness," ask the next question: "What's a *truer* thought?" Once a different, more accurate thought is created, ask for supporting evidence, or examples, that support this new thought.

I often used the Thought Lie Detector Approach with my daughter, especially when she was very worried about something. Aly wasn't the kind of child who would always volunteer to talk about what was bothering her, unless it got to what I called "the critical boiling point," when she would tell me she couldn't fall asleep and she seemed distracted or got unusually quiet. When I would tell her that she seemed not to be herself and ask her what was wrong, it would usually come pouring out of her like an erupting volcano. Initially, I would just listen and let her vent her feelings and thoughts about what was bothering her. Afterward, I would go through the series of questions discussed above to help her recognize how the thoughts she was having were not true and the "story" she was creating was equally untrue. When she realized that these thoughts were not true, it was an amazing thing to watch. Her face and body would relax, and it was as if a light bulb had gone on in her head, illuminating the reality of her thoughts. Her breathing changed, her smile came back, and she looked as if a huge weight had been lifted from her. That's what truthful thoughts can do for us!

For years, I used the Thought Lie Detector Approach with Aly to give her the tools to deal with untrue thoughts. As I helped Aly deal with thoughts that caused her emotional pain, I used the same approach with myself. I realized how much my thoughts controlled my behavior and the actions I took as a result of them. Thoughts like, "If I don't let Aly have that dress she wants, she'll be angry and not love me" resulted in me giving in to her request and then unfairly treating her like she was spoiled. Or, with my husband Jeff, "I shouldn't have lost my temper, because now he'll be in a bad mood and he'll ignore me," which made me feel rejected and even angrier at him. These kinds of thoughts have a way of creating a screenplay for an inner movie that always has a sad ending. When I realized that my untrue thoughts were causing the pain I felt inside, I also recognized that I had the power to reverse the anger, sadness, or fear I felt by changing my thoughts, which would let me see the situations in my life from a "truer," and more fulfilling, vantage point.

Along the way, I also discovered a process similar to the Thought Lie Detector Approach, but more in depth. I heartily recommend Byron Katie's excellent book about thought inquiry, *Loving What Is.* In the book, Katie describes the steps that stopped her suffering from chronic depression, emotional upheaval, and a life that was painful and created a life that brought her peace and joy. Her approach, called The Work, consists of a four-question inquiry and turnaround process:

1. Is it true?

2. Can you absolutely know that it's true?

3. How do you react when you think that thought?

4. Who would you be without that thought?

The last part of the inquiry process is called the turnaround, in which you rewrite the original thought statement. For example: "He never loved me for who I am" gets rewritten and replaced with "I," as in, "I never loved myself for who I am." Another type of turnaround is when a thought statement becomes its polar opposite. There could be several turnarounds for each thought statement; the goal is to determine whether the turnaround statement is as true or more true than your original statement. For each turnaround, you come up with examples that support it. The simplicity of The Work allows us to really question and investigate stressful thoughts. Children as well as adults can benefit immensely from this type of inquiry approach. It allows us to expand our minds and learn not to accept untrue thoughts that stop us from finding peace and understanding and from being self-loving.

It is important to help your child learn that his thoughts are as natural as rain falling or wind blowing. We cannot control the number of thoughts that are created; we can only work on learning to understand them. The power of our thoughts can affect the way our body feels. When we have positive thoughts, our brain releases chemicals that slow our breathing, relax our muscles, and create an overall sense of well-being. Conversely, negative and untrue thoughts give us headaches, uneasy stomachs, tight muscles, and a sense of gloom and doom. These thoughts contaminate and sabotage behaviors that are loving to ourselves. When we realize that thoughts can be changed, we experience freedom and the ability to choose "truer" thoughts, thoughts that are more aligned with that "inner spark" of love with which we were born.

♡ Heartfelt Points to Remember

♡ Our brain produces thousands of thoughts a day, many of them automatic negative thoughts.

♡ Negative thoughts or beliefs are not hurtful or harmful unless we get attached to them and believe they are true without questioning them.

♡ Learn to change habitual negative thought processes by simply questioning them before they can produce painful, unloving repercussions.

♡ Use the Thought Lie Detector Approach or The Work to challenge untrue negative thoughts and create "truer" ones to replace them.

♡ Thoughts are as natural as rain falling or wind blowing. Since we cannot control the number of thoughts that are created, we can only hope to learn to understand them.

Creating Our Best Choices

Everybody, sooner or later, sits down to a banquet of consequences.

~ROBERT LOUIS STEVENSON

Dear Aly,

You are old enough now to see the consequences of not loving yourself. How many times did you sit in your health class and listen to discussions about drug and alcohol overdose, anorexia, bullying, teen pregnancy, depression, and suicide? These topics are not always pleasant to talk about, especially when you can see how easily any one of these things could happen.

Aly, I know that there have been times in your life when you have been faced with making decisions that have caused you angst. That anxiety comes from worries about what will happen when you make that decision and the consequences that result from it. Do you remember when you were fifteen and I asked you to decide whether to go on a summer teen tour? The tour was with a group of kids you didn't know, and it was totally out of your comfort zone. You cried, you complained, and you were angry, but deep down you sensed it was something that you had to do. That "deep down" sense was you tuning into what was the most loving thing for you to do in order to grow as a person. You sensed that learning to be on your own in a safe setting, learning to make friends who were not from your school, and dealing with being away from home might turn out to be beneficial or maybe even fun. And you were right! The trip was one of the most pivotal experiences of your teenage years. The child I left at the airport (who clung to me as we said our goodbyes) was not the same person I picked up three weeks later. I watched, thrilled, as you happily came off the plane, hugging all of your newfound friends and feeling confident and self-assured. That's what making loving decisions for yourself feels like!

As we work on the thoughts that cause us emotional pain, we need to understand how to make the wise decisions that will lead us to prudent actions. The simplest decision-making approach arises from two questions that you ask yourself before you make a decision: "Is this (action, thought, or relationship) the most loving to me (or to others)?" If the answer is "no", then ask yourself the next question: What are the most loving things I can do for myself (or for others) in this situation? It sounds so simple, doesn't it?

Aly, it took me years to learn that the simplest way is often the most powerful. These questions work like a compass, leading you back to what I call your "true north." After you ask yourself the questions— whether it be about going to a party at college, being in a relationship with someone, or taking any action that you are unsure of, if the answer comes back a resounding "no," and you see those red flags, then stop and make the decision based on other loving things you could do in that situation. Sometimes when we get that "no" answer, we may not want to heed it, but in the long run, the actions or behaviors that are the most loving to us are also the truest and best for us.

As you go off to college in the fall and are faced with situations that only you can solve or decide, remember to ask yourself that loving question to guide you. It will be your true north, and it will help you continue to love yourself through your life. My greatest wish is that you let it be your constant, truest companion as you move into adulthood.

Love,
Mommy

*h*ave you ever wondered why some children succumb to behaviors or actions that are harmful to them and others do not? Many factors influence children's actions, including parental involvement, societal pressures, psychological factors, physical brain development, heredity, and morality. There are several ways that children learn what I call their "code of living," the paradigm that encompasses their appropriate behaviors and ways of interacting with the world around them. Most parents strive to teach their children core values that reflect the family's beliefs about right and wrong. As children mature and interact more with the "outside world," schools, religious institutions, sports teams, child and teen organizations, and specified educational programs also encourage and teach children how to conduct themselves and how to learn to make the right choices in life. Yet if you were taught—or "reminded"—how to love yourself, might that be the one difference that would change the equation of all of those other factors? I believe it can be. Loving ourselves can lead us to make positive choices in our lives.

So what are the consequences when we "forget" to love ourselves? As a parent, there have been times when my own child chose a different path from the one that I, as an adult, would have chosen for her. My first instinct was usually to blame the temporal part of her brain for not being totally wired or developed yet, making her more impulsive. But was there something else going on there? I came to realize that there is a "forgetting" and then a "remembering" process that may occur along the path of learning to love oneself. As Dr. Gay Hendricks described this phenomenon in his book *Learning to Love Yourself,* "You will forget to love yourself until the very last moment, then you will remember again, only to forget again, and remember. And it does not matter because the essential transformation takes place at the moment you are *willing* to love. Being willing to love ourselves means that we are greeting life with acceptance rather than resistance." How can we help "remind" our children of this, especially when they are learning to make decisions in their lives about certain actions, behavioral or relational, that will affect them? The following exercise is one that I have found to be helpful in triggering the memory of that loving spark within. That loving inner spark is the best compass; it leads us to make wise choices and create successful subsequent actions. When we follow the "directions" of our inner spark, we are always guided to the right place. I have taught my daughter and others to use this exercise, and I have incorporated it into my own life every day.

♡ Love to Exercise 8 ♡

The Love Compass

In teaching children, and even ourselves, how to figure out what is the most loving choice in any decision, we need to create a "trigger," or a set of questions that can help us remember and guide us to what is loving to us.

When your child or teen is in the process of contemplating a certain action, thought pattern, or relationship that will have consequences, both positive or negative, have them ask the Love Compass' two simple yet powerful questions:

Question 1: Is this (action, thought pattern, or relationship) the most loving to me (or to others)?

Example 1: A seven-year-old boy is being pressured by his peers to steal a classmate's, Johnny's, lunch as a prank. The question to be asked is: "Is taking Johnny's lunch the most loving to me or to Johnny?"

Example 2: A twelve-year-old girl spends a long time thinking about how she thinks the size of her nose makes her look ugly. The question to be asked is: "Is continuing to focus on how I think my nose makes me look ugly the most loving to me?"

Example 3: A seventeen-year-old girl is upset with her boyfriend, Brandon, who keeps cheating on her. The question to be asked is: "Is being in this relationship with Brandon the most loving to me?"

If the answer to the first question is "no," then the next thing to do is ask the second important question:

Question 2: What are the most loving things I can do for myself (or for others) in this situation?

Make a list of at least three things that would be the most loving things to do in the situation. It may be a mental list, or you may choose to write it down. When doing this exercise with younger children, help them by counting on your fingers the three options they come up with, or make a chart so they can visually see their options.

Let's use Example 3 to illustrate the importance of the second question. If the girl's answer to the first question is "no," the second question will help her come up with wise choices that will outline the most loving course of action. For example, the

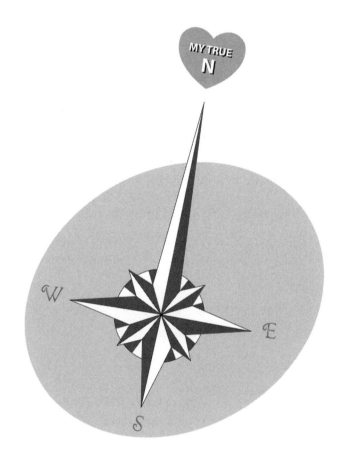

The Love Compass

three most loving things this teen might do for herself in her relationship with Brandon include:

1. Talk to him about her feelings and see if he responds to them in an understanding manner.

2. Believe that she deserves someone who is honorable and truthful in relationships, like she is.

3. Accept that his core values do not match hers and end the relationship.

The two questions in this exercise are important prompts that can produce a path back to the recognition of that inner knowledge of self-love. The Love Compass is an easy approach that can give us the right "directions" for how to proceed in life. I like to say that it leads us to our "true north." The first question gives us the opportunity to pause and "remember" that inner spark once again. The second question takes it one step further, eliciting loving options as guideposts that enable us to take prudent actions as a result of these suggestions. The Love Compass does not only have to be used in negative situations, however. It can also reinforce loving choices that we make for ourselves. Children learn by repetition, and the more that these two simple and potent questions are used in their everyday life, the more they become part of their repertoire in contemplating their behavior.

Sometimes finding loving choices means that those choices we originally made may on the surface seem like the "wrong" ones. However, in the end they may prove to be powerful lessons that help us learn and grow as individuals. I think we can all remember instances in our lives when we made decisions that we regret, but in retrospect those decisions became a catalyst for major changes in our lives. Often it is not the action we took but what we learned from the consequences of it that matters. When a child or teen is able to glean from an experience what aspects would be loving to them, it sets in motion the "remembering" aspect of self-love. Whether it's learning how to question untrue thoughts or learning what are the most loving actions children can take in their lives, it all boils down to attaching love to our actions and opening up more opportunities to express it. And isn't that what we all want for our children?

♡Heartfelt Points to Remember

♡ Loving ourselves is a powerful dynamic that can lead us to make positive choices in our lives, whether in relationships or in how we treat ourselves and others.

♡ There is a "forgetting" and then "remembering" process that sometimes occurs in the path of learning to love ourselves.

♡ Use the Love Compass questions to help produce the most loving and caring choices that can lead to positive consequences.

♡ Children learn by repetition, and the more they use the Love Compass' simple and potent questions in their everyday life, the more these questions will become part of their repertoire in contemplating their behavior.

♡ Learning from the consequences of an experience and the loving aspects of what was learned can set in motion the "remembering" aspect of self-love.

Living Loving Kindness

Bring Back That Lovin' Feeling

Love yourself first and everything else falls into line.
You really have to love yourself to get anything done in
this world.

~LUCILLE BALL

Dear Aly,

While you and I were packing boxes and suitcases getting you ready for college, it gave me time to reflect about you and my role in your life. If packing wasn't emotional enough, I found myself flashing back to your infancy, early childhood, school years, and adolescence, with me being one of the central influences in the "movie of your life." I never, ever imagined as your Mommy/Guide/Protector/Disciplinarian that I would learn so much from you when I thought I was supposed to be teaching you! I had the great joy of learning to view life through your eyes, and enjoy being in the moment, to smile and laugh more, and most importantly, I learned to love myself. Yes, as I found ways to teach you this important life lesson, I, too, began living those principles as well. What a gift you gave me!

Looking back, I realize that the path to loving oneself is an ongoing journey that will never stop. Many experiences in your life will remind you of this, and some of those experiences will challenge what you know is the right choice and try to pull you away from your "true north," that place of self-love. But you'll be able to find the path back by remembering the inner spark of love that you were born with, and you'll keep nurturing that love so it will only get brighter. Once you have experienced internal appreciation, love within, it will continue to grow and will never truly be forgotten. It's not like a history test that you pull an all-nighter for, cramming all that information into your brain, only to forget it once the test is over. No, Aly, once the imprint of loving yourself is uncovered, there's no going back, and it only gets better and better!

Over the years, Dad and I have had the great pleasure of uncovering this seed of love—watering it, nourishing it, and watching it unfold within you. Now, you are old enough to take over this responsibility, allowing it to continue to grow and expand. The best way to do this is to practice loving kindness to yourself. Simply put, please BE KIND TO YOURSELF, ALY! Give yourself all that you need to be happy and healthy. Cheer yourself up when you are sad or lonely. Eat well, and do things that are good for your body. Say nice things to yourself just as you would say to a good friend. Aly, use those four little words—be kind to yourself—to remind yourself that you are worthy and deserving of loving kindness, goodness, and all the things that make you feel good about yourself.

The best way to remember to be kind to yourself is to practice, practice, practice! So when you are walking to class, or waiting in line for your afternoon Chai latte, remind yourself to do one act of kindness for yourself. Maybe it's going to the gym or going to bed early to catch up on some needed sleep, or being able to recognize those negative, untrue thoughts about not being smart enough to figure out what to write on your upcoming English paper. Whatever it is, depending on what your needs are each day, being kind to yourself creates those loving actions in your life that help remind you how deserving you are of love. It is the act of loving kindness that keeps that inner spark ignited. And, by the way, when we practice loving kindness to ourselves, not only are we able to be more loving toward others, we also feel energized and joyful.

As your parent, your mom, and someone who has been your caregiver every day for the last eighteen years, I know that you are ready to make that big leap into the next exciting phase in your life—leaving home for the first time and going to college. How do I know that? Well, moms have a kind of sixth sense with which we can perceive things about our children, even without them saying or doing anything to clue us in. I can also sense your trepidation about leaving, and I feel you wanting to hang on to every precious moment of feeling protected by your house, your dogs, and those close to you. I know that you have the strength to conquer and embrace this newest adventure in your life and the skills to help you move along this wondrous highway called life. Just remember the mantra "I love me," hug yourself every day, find the truth behind those untrue and fear-based thoughts, ask what actions are loving to you, and practice loving kindness to yourself each and every day. It all starts and ends with that four-letter word called L-O-V-E. I love you with all my heart . . .

Love,
Mommy

*W*here did the words *loving kindness* originate? In 1535, Myles Coverdale coined the biblical wordphrase "louinge kyndnesse" for his Coverdale Bible as an English translation for the Hebrew word *chesed,* meaning "kindness." During medieval times, knights considered kindness to be one of their supreme virtues. Loving kindness is also an English equivalent for the Buddhist term *metta,* which represents one of the "parimitas" (the ten imperfections) and is often used in a meditation. There is no doubt that kindness and love are highly esteemed in various religions and ideologies. Most parents want their children to aspire to kindness. However, combining love and kindness in the context of self-love gives it a slightly different connotation. It means that we turn that kindness inward, toward ourselves.

Aristotle claimed that kindness led to the desire to help another in need, unconditionally, without expecting anything in return. Unfortunately, human beings often seem to find it easier to be kind to others than to ourselves. Perhaps this is because when we see someone in pain, the visual picture of his or her suffering registers in our brain. Yet when it comes to our own pain, we can't often see the pain with our eyes, and we forget that the same kindness and care that we extend to others must be extended inward. Parents and caregivers strive to teach children to show kindness toward others through sharing, comforting their friends when they are hurt or sad, and being compassionate to those who are less fortunate. However, when our children utter unkind comments about themselves or create experiences that are detrimental to them, we don't necessarily teach them that kindness starts with ourselves and radiates outward to others.

You, yourself, as much as anybody in the entire universe, deserve your love and affection.

~ Buddha

The first step in helping children learn loving kindness toward themselves is to help them understand what loving kindness is. What does being kind to yourself feel like? What does it look like? Explain that being kind to yourself means not beating yourself up with untrue, fear-based thoughts; being in relationships that are meaningful; learning from past decisions or actions and doing things differently the second time around; doing nurturing things for oneself everyday; and honoring your body by taking good care of it. For most children, it also means learning to turn off the nagging critic that sits on their shoulder, telling them what's wrong with them instead of appreciating all the wonderful aspects of their very being. Living loving kindness is like taking baby steps every day— one small, loving gesture at a time.

Children learn that being kind to themselves develops patience, acceptance, and recognizing and valuing their own needs. The way parents can cultivate that inner spark of love within each of their children is to help them practice the art of living loving kindness each day. Just like the title of this chapter, *Bring Back That Lovin' Feeling,* we need to create that "lovin' feeling" by practicing loving kindness to ourselves. This is something that we don't often teach our children, let alone do for ourselves. One of the best ways to teach our brains new strategies is repetition. When you practice inward loving kindness every day, it becomes a habit and becomes part of your daily repertoire. When children learn to express loving kindness toward themselves, it becomes much easier for them to show loving kindness and compassion toward others. The ultimate goal for children is to be able to do both equally.

♡ **Love to Exercise 9** ♡

There are different versions of this exercise for children in different age groups. The end result will be the same: learning to practice inward-facing loving kindness. As a parent, feel free to modify any of the following exercises for yourself to experience what living loving kindness feels like.

♡ The Loving Kindness Wish(es) for the Day (preschool–age 10)

In a jar or a bowl with a lid, put strips of paper on which your child and/or you have written fun, loving activities for your child to do for himself every day. On one side of the paper, describe the loving kindness activity, and on the back explain why this activity is a loving kindness to the child. Have him select one or more of these strips each day from the Loving Kindness Jar. To create a visual picture of living loving kindness each day, place a monthly calendar in his room or in a place where he spends a lot of time, and put stars on the days that he lives loving kindness toward himself. Examples:

1. Take a bubble bath and fill the tub up with your favorite bath toys.
   Reason: This loving kindness is helping our bodies keep clean and have fun in the water.

2. Name three things that make you special and unique.
   Reason: This loving kindness is a reminder of who you really are and ignites that inner loving spark within.

3. Give yourself a big hug, smile, and sing, "I love me."
   Reason: This loving kindness is a way to show how much you love yourself.

♡ Daily L K 2 Me (11–18 years old)

The adolescent years can be unsettling ones, even for the most confident kids, due to the many developmental and physiological changes occurring within. Reminding teens and preteens to practice loving kindness toward themselves will help smooth out those sometimes turbulent days they may experience at this age.

Here are some ideas to help this age group learn to live loving kindness:

1. *Create a screen saver:* Have your teen or preteen create a screen saver on her computer that says "Every Day Live Loving Kindness to Myself and Others." It's a subtle, unconscious way for her to see the message everyday.

2. *A Loving Kindness Calendar:* Buy a blank calendar and give it to your teen, with instructions that each day he must fill in a "Daily L K 2 Me" act that he completes, either for himself or for others. Activities can be simple things like: take a bike ride (exercising your body), name three things that you enjoy about yourself (reinforcing the positive aspects about yourself), eat healthy snacks (promotes healthy diet), or watch a relaxing movie/TV show after doing homework (supports balance of hard work and relaxation). At the end of the week, a parent can ask to see the calendar to find out what loving kindness actions he chose for himself and for others. To reinforce this exercise, use praise such as "You must feel

really proud of yourself for treating yourself (or others) with so much loving kindness! Good job!"

3. *A Loving Kindness Memory Board:* Buy a corkboard that can be placed by your teen's desk or in a convenient place so that she will constantly see it. Ask her to fill the board with pictures of loving kindness actions that she can imagine doing for herself and for others from magazines or from other printed material. She may also want to add Post-It Notes of loving kindness ideas that she thinks of on her own. Whenever she completes a loving kindness action from the board, have her put a star on the picture or Post-It so she can see how many LK actions she completed for herself.

A parent's role is to guide and prepare a child for life, but when we embarked on this wondrous journey called parenthood, we were not handed an instruction manual. We all want our children to be successful—in school, in their friendships, and in any endeavor that they choose to pursue. To achieve this goal, we end up reading countless books or articles on parenting; enroll our children in clubs, activities, and schools; and do whatever else is out there to promote a sense of achievement and accomplishment for them. But even with all of this, there is no guarantee that our greatest wishes for them will come true. Yet the one thing—so simple, so pure, and so right—that can ensure inner happiness for our children is to help them uncover and be aware of the love within each one of them. By helping our children tap into their birthright of love, we help them learn to embrace themselves—with all of their strengths and flaws.

They learn that when they truly cherish themselves, it is not being self-centered or egotistical or succumbing to selfish, destructive behaviors, but valuing themselves and having the ability to give their love freely without fear. It's not about having to be the best-looking, the most talented, or the one who has the most possessions. It is about honoring that powerful universal force called love within that creates compassion, joy, peace, and true fulfillment. The road map to loving themselves is the one gift that all parents can give their children that will always sustain, nurture, and envelop them as they move through the roller coaster of life!

Heartfelt Points to Remember

♡ Living loving kindness through the context of self-love means to turn that kindness inward.

♡ Help children equate and understand that kindness starts with ourselves and then radiates outward to others.

♡ Children learn that being kind to themselves develops patience, acceptance, and recognizing and valuing their own needs.

♡ By practicing inward loving kindness every day, it becomes a habit, which will then become part of a child's daily repertoire.

♡ The ultimate goal for children is to be able to *equally* express loving kindness toward themselves and to show loving kindness and compassion toward others.

Epilogue

Checking the arrivals board at the airport, I see that Aly's flight has just landed. It's Thanksgiving break, and she is coming home from college for the first time. As I anxiously wait for her, I flash back to the two days we spent helping Aly move into her dorm room just a few months ago, marking the start of her freshman year.

> *Our rented van was filled to the brim with boxes, suitcases, and other dorm room paraphernalia. We waited in a long line of cars that looked just like ours to unload and begin the arduous task of moving all the "stuff" into her small dorm room. Aly gazed out her window with a pensive look on her face as we waited.*
>
> *"You all right back there?" I asked.*
>
> *Turning her head and looking at us, she softly whispered, "I just can't believe I'm really here. I've been thinking about this moment, and now I'm really going to live in a dorm and be in college. So many things right now feel so new. I think I'll be okay, but how do I know for sure?"*

Suddenly, my daughter's voice brings me back to the present. There she is, walking toward me, with that beautiful smile of hers. "Mom," she says, "it's sooo great to see you!" And we embrace each other in a long, overdue hug. As much as we have stayed in touch with phone calls and video chats, there is nothing like holding "my baby" in my arms! She and I put her luggage in the trunk, and we start our drive back home where her father and her dogs happily await her return.

Even though we have spoken regularly over the past few months, watching her face as she animatedly tells me about everything all at once, I begin to get a true sense of who my daughter is becoming. Her descriptions of her teachers and classes, her appreciation of her roommates and other newfound friends, her exciting new social life—acceptance into a sorority (and boys!)—allow me to gauge how well my daughter is doing in her new life as a college student. Glancing at her as she speaks, I begin to see that Aly is different. The girl that was looking out the window as we drove up to her dorm is not the same as the girl sitting next to me now. It is evident that she's blossoming into a confident, self-assured young woman.

The question she asked in the car with a bit of a quiver in her voice—"How do I know for sure?"—has been answered. The gift of reminding her of the inner spark of love that she brought with her into this world over the years has taught her to truly love herself. I can hear in her conversation (or I should say monologue!) that the decisions she has already made in this short period of time reflect that she does understand that love is her birthright and that she will treat it and herself with respect and commitment. She now knows she will be okay. Her newly found confidence, her greater ability to make good choices when faced with new situations, her ever-growing independence, and her ability to assess her relationships are sure signs that she took what I taught her about loving herself and is now able to reflect that into her world. And I couldn't be happier!

Dr. Andie and daughter Aly, 2010

Appendix
Blue Chip Interview Questions

For babysitters, teachers, and other caregivers

1. What adjectives would you use to describe yourself?

2. Whether it's a historical figure, movie star, author, or anyone else you look up to, who is your role model? Why?

3. What do you think the ingredients are for children to become successful in life?

4. What qualities do you possess that lead you to work with children?

5. What is your philosophy on praise and discipline?

6. Describe one of your favorite experiences you've had with children.

Recommended Resources

Books

NurtureShock: New Thinking About Children, by Po Bronson and Ashley Merryman (12 Group, New York, 2009).

Baby Hearts: A Guide to Giving Your Child an Emotional Head Start, by Linda Acredolo, Ph.D., and Susan Goodwyn, Ph.D. (Bantam Books, New York, 2005).

The Girl's Guide to Loving Yourself, by Diane Mastromarino (Blue Mountain Arts, Boulder, Colorado, 2003).

Learning to Love Yourself: A Guide to Becoming Centered, by Gay Hendricks, Ph.D. (Simon & Schuster, New York, 1993).

Loving Yourself: Four Steps to a Happier You, by Daphne Rose Kingma (Conari Press, San Francisco, 2004).

Evolve Your Brain: The Science of Changing Your Mind, by Joe Dispenza, D.C. (Health Communications, Inc., Deerfield, Florida, 2007).

Change Your Brain, Change Your Life, by Daniel G. Amen, M.D. (Three Rivers Press, New York, 1998).

What's Going On in There? How the Brain and Mind Develop in the First Five Years of Life, by Lise Elliot, Ph.D. (Bantam Books, New York, 2000).

Loving What Is: Four Questions That Can Change Your Life, by Byron Katie with Stephen Mitchell (Three Rivers Press, New York, 2002).

The Best Investment: Unlocking the Secrets of Social Success for Your Child, by Andrea Goodman Weiner, Ed.D. (Emotionally Smart Beginnings, Holicong, PA, 2008).

The Biology of Belief: Unleashing the Power of Consciousness, Matter and Miracles, by Bruce Lipton, Ph.D. (Elite Books, Santa Rosa, CA, 2005).

Websites

www.kalimunro.com/tips_self-love.html

www.4therapy.com/consumer/life_topics/article/6713/489/
    Learning+to+love+yourself

www.marsvenusliving.com/2009/08/12/love-yourself/

www.parentingscience.com/effects-of-praise.html

www.ehow.com/how_8431_talk-baby-utero.html

www.associatedcontent.com/article/280401/how_do_babies_
    learn_pg2.html?cat=25

www.developmental-psychology.suite101.com/article.cfm/
    unconditional_love

www.yourbabytoday.com/features/brainpower/index.html

About the Author

Dr. Andrea "Andie" Weiner has concentrated her research on children's social and emotional skill development for over twenty-five years. As founder of Emotionally Smart Beginnings, she produces educational products for children and parents that cover topics from making friends to how to read emotional cues.

After spending several years as a child and family therapist at Hahnemann University (Tenet Health Systems), she served as Vice President of Medical Delivery Systems at US Healthcare/Aetna, where she developed mental health programs for subscribers.

Dr. Andie worked in schools presenting self-esteem projects in classrooms as well as coaching teachers on using new, innovative strategies addressing social skills for students. Her multiple careers as child therapist, psycho-educational specialist, business executive, and author and lecturer—as well as mother—have enabled her to develop a wealth of experience and insight on how social and emotional skills can create lifelong benefits.

Her first book, *The Best Investment: Unlocking the Secrets of Social Success for Your Child,* has been praised by parents and educators all over the country for its easy readability and the powerful, yet simple strategies that parents and other caregivers can easily implement with great results that last a lifetime. She is a popular guest on radio and television talk shows nationwide and a prolific lecturer and speaker. She lives in Bucks County, Pennsylvania, with her husband, Jeffery, and their daughter, Aly. You can write to her at Dr.Andie@drandie.com, or to arrange lectures and workshops call 888-553-0235 or email newsworthy@sansoneplus.com.

www.drandie.com